OPERATION BROGUE

TO
THOSE IRISH JOURNALISTS
WHO
DESPITE INDUCEMENT AND PRESSURE
TOLD THE WHOLE TRUTH
TO
THE IRISH PEOPLE

Operation Brogue

A Study of the Vilification
of Charles Haughey
Code-named 'Operation Brogue'
by the British Secret Service

JOHN M. FEEHAN

*The height of a man is not measured from his head to the ground
but from his head to the sky.*
– NAPOLEON BONAPARTE

THE MERCIER PRESS
DUBLIN and CORK

The Mercier Press Limited
4 Bridge Street, Cork
24 Lower Abbey Street, Dublin 1

Feehan, John M.
    Operation Brogue: A study of the vilification of Charles J. Haughey code-
    named Operation Brogue by the British Secret Service.
    1. Haughey, Charles J.
    I. Title
    941.70824'092'4   DA965.H3

    ISBN 0-85342-729-1

Books by the same author:

AN IRISH PUBLISHER AND HIS WORLD
TOMORROW TO BE BRAVE
THE WIND THAT ROUND THE FASTNET SWEEPS
THE MAGIC OF THE KERRY COAST
THE MAGIC OF THE SHANNON
THE IRISH BEDSIDE BOOK
THE SHOOTING OF MICHAEL COLLINS
BOBBY SANDS AND THE TRAGEDY OF NORTHERN IRELAND

Contents

Introduction

*The laws of writing command us to rise above our anger
and try to see the present in the light of eternity.*
— ALEXANDER SOLZHENITSYN

In this book I tried to show that sections of the media have been unfair to Mr Haughey by presenting an unfavourable one-sided picture. I tried to present the *other* side of this picture in such a way that the Irish public will then have seen *both* sides and can make up their minds for themselves. I have also suggested areas where the media might investigate more fully in order that the people may be able to come to better and more mature judgments. This book, therefore, is not an attempt to answer various criticisms levelled at Charles Haughey in the past. I tried to state the truth as I saw it whether or not it shocks prevailing opinion. I am not a judge, but simply a communicator. I am not trying to score one over anybody or anything. I merely tried to show the public that there *is* another side.

We sometimes forget that 'Freedom of the Press' has a two-fold meaning. Firstly, it means that the ordinary reading public have the right and the freedom to obtain the whole truth and not slanted or distorted versions, and secondly it means that journalists are free from censorship. Any breach of either of these two elements is a breach of 'Freedom of the Press'.

I have had to take a special look at the murky, dirty area of the activities of the British Secret Service in this campaign against Charles Haughey. I did not find out as much as I had hoped. Almost everywhere I turned I came up against blank walls but each wall had a little chink and in this way I got enough of a glimpse to tell me that I was on the right track and that there was a sinister world of deceit, intrigue, falsehood and double-dealing which was carefully concealed from us. I did, however, find out that there *was* a plan, with almost unlimited funds behind it, to split Fianna Fáil and destroy Charlie Haughey. Like all other special British Secret Service operations it was given a code-name – OPERATION BROGUE.

In the course of this book we will take a close look at the over-all British plan for Ireland. OPERATION BROGUE is an important element within that plan. When the British tried to get rid of Dr Mossadeq in Iran they code-named the plan OPERATION BOOT. Their sardonic humour seems to suggest that they use some word for BOOT in their code, presumably because it conjures up the act of kicking out.

The objective of OPERATION BROGUE was to work towards getting a government into power, either Fine Gael or Fianna Fáil, that would co-operate with British military war aims. Beyond that I was unable to penetrate very far, but I was certainly intrigued by the fact that the British believed they could find within Fianna Fáil a leader upon whom they could depend. They were, however, quite clear that Charles Haughey was *not* that leader. They assessed him as a man too close to the original aims of Fianna Fáil to be of any use to them, or to do their bidding.

The reason I have called this book OPERATION BROGUE is that I am satisfied that the British Secret Service were the original instigators of the campaign of vilification against him. Metaphorically speaking, they created the snow while others unwittingly threw the snowballs. Many people opposed Mr Haughey and criticised him severely in the belief they were doing the country a justice, whereas without knowing it, they could have been aiding the British plan to destroy him.

I followed the same method I used in my last two books *The Shooting of Michael Collins* and *Bobby Sands and the Tragedy of Northern Ireland,* namely I concerned myself with *realpolitik,* with substance, not with shadow. *Realpolitik* is a German word which, literally translated means *the politics of reality.* It was widely practised by Bismarck and successive German statesmen and it took the form of giving priority to real material advantage and not to ideals, which were seen as something to be exploited to achieve political ends. Simply put, a *realpolitik* attitude is one that looks at the sayings and doings of politicians with a strong and healthy scepticism.

I should also like to clarify three other points which are of considerable importance. The first is: what I understand by *violence?* Unfortunately many writers fail to clarify what they mean by that word. The best definition I know is that of the great South American Archbishop, Dom Helder Camera. Archbishop Camera shows that violence has three *indivisible tiers: The Violence of Injustice, The Violence of Reaction,* and *Institutional Violence.*

Injustice in itself, in any state, is a major act of violence. This in turn produces the second tier, the reaction of the oppressed to injustice, which in turn produces the third tier – the reaction of the security forces to the second tier. It is, of course, a waste of time trying to eliminate the second or third tier while the first still exists. Contrarywise, eliminate the first tier and you automatically eliminate the other two. In the Irish context, there-fore, the real men of violence are the first tier, namely, the British and those who actively support them. This is the harsh *realpolitik,* whether we like it or not, and no amount of quibbling can change that.

The second point of importance I would like to mention con-cerns the eagerness in the past of certain critics to put words in my mouth which I never uttered. While they admitted I did not say certain things, they suggested I 'implied' them. I want to make it clear that I say what I say, and I 'imply' nothing.

This book does not in any way imply or suggest or insinuate that those who oppose Mr Haughey, or who have written, spoken or acted against him, are disloyal to their country and are knowingly promoting the British cause in Ireland or are part of OPERATION BROGUE. They must be credited with acting according to their lights and doing the job of work given to them in the best way they see possible.* Here and there throughout the book I may criticise people's behaviour or actions. I am, however, not criticising their worth. I have tried to make Solzhenitsyn's quotation at the head of this Introduction my guiding light.

Thirdly, where I use the word 'British' in this book I mean in essence that section known as 'The British Establishment' which deserves the worst anyone can say of it and whose attitude towards Ireland has not changed in two hundred and fifty years. I do not mean the ordinary decent British citizens. Nor do I mean those wonderful Britons who campaign, day in day out, in the cause of justice and peace, and who are in the very best traditions of William Cobbett, John Wilkes, Tom Paine, George Orwell and Claud Cockburn.

* *These remarks, of course, apply also to critics of others in the public eye.*

In writing this book, I spoke with well over one hundred people and, as in the case of my other books, I refused and still refuse point blank to reveal their identities. This may seem irritating to some few readers but for a writer it has one wonderful advantage – people trust him again and again knowing that he will not expose them.

One individual, however, I did not interview was Mr Haughey. When I told him I was writing this book, he very kindly offered to give me any help he could. Without being disrespectful or ungracious in any way, I declined his kind offer, because I felt, since he was the central character, it would be better if I used other sources. I can, therefore, make the negative statement that nothing in this book came from Mr Haughey himself.

I do not write from the standpoint of any political party. I am not and have never been a member of one. I am an Irish nationalist who believes in a free and independent thirty-two county republic, and as I get older I have come to see clearly that the greatest single evil in the history of Ireland, past, present and future, is British interference in the affairs of our country and the co-operation by Irishmen in this interference. It has cost millions of Irish lives and might well cost millions more in the future. I offer no apology to anyone for that outlook. It is not 'hard-line'. It is simply the outlook of any man who loves his country and his people.

I want to thank especially a number of journalists who helped me in the sense that I found much in their writings of great assistance. As well as the main newspapers, I found the various monthly magazines similarly helpful. And again a special word of thanks to the editors of *The Mercier Press* for their painstaking work on the final manuscript.

And finally a word of thanks to my lawyers who were particularly helpful.

Go mba fada buan iad go leir.

J. M. F.

1: British War Aims

It would be difficult to understand fully the recent attempts to destroy Charles Haughey without taking a look at the broader background into which these extraordinary events were set. Completely dominating that broader background is the role Britain has played, and is playing, in the affairs of this country. To examine that background is not as easy as it appears at first sight. In recent decades the teaching of Irish history has been distorted to the point where one has to dig hard to find the truth.

In the 1960s in Ireland, as well as the hula-hoop, side burns, long hair and narrow trousers, there came upon the scene another fad which was destined to carry itself over to the present day but which, like all fads, is fading rapidly. This fad came to be known as 'revisionist history'. Many of these new faddists began to teach and write history by not overburdening their brains too much with its important episodes as they actually happened, but by interpreting these events in a way which was very much at variance with reality.

Their main theme was that those historians who went before them seriously misunderstood Irish history. The English were not our enemies. They were actually acting in our best interest but we did not appreciate it. The millions they slaughtered and

starved to death were, after all, subversives who were disturbing
the peace and who, without doubt, deserved their fate. All
round we should be grateful to the English for the considerate
care they showered upon us since they first came to our country
to help us. After all, these historians argued, one must be
modern and up-to-date. One must forget the United Ireland
mentality which was only a sign of backwardness in a modern
pluralist Ireland.

Many of these teachers and writers overlooked the fact that
were it not for the 'terrorists' and the 'subversives' they would
probably still be hewers of wood and drawers of water. It did
not occur to them to resign from their well paid positions because
these positions came about as the result of an effective combina-
tion of the rifle and the ballot box. Shakespeare probably put
the best description of many of them into the mouth of Iago:

> . . . duteous and knee-crooking knave
> that doting on his own obsequious bondage
> weans out his time much like his master's ass
> for naught but provender.

Nevertheless it would be wrong to conclude that twenty-five
years of this kind of obsequious teaching did not have some
effect. It went part of the way towards creating, in an otherwise
intelligent people, the type of British mind in which a man of
Haughey's Republican beliefs could be vilified with a reasonable
hope of success.

If, however, we try to search out the truth and concentrate
on the *realpolitik,* we will come face to face with two searching
questions which have to be answered if we are to make any
headway.

The first of those questions is: *What is Britain's real interest
in Ireland?* That question is fundamental to any understanding
of modern Ireland and to answer it properly we must go back
briefly to the beginning of the conquest.

It is probably reasonable to say that in those far off days the
English were simply plunderers seeking new land and in Ireland
they found what they wanted, a politically, though not culturally
or spiritually, disunited nation. By playing one faction off against
the other, much the same as they do today, they managed to
gain a substantial foothold.

It was only after the Reformation when England began to expand as a world power and take the first steps in invading other nations that the real conquest of Ireland began. This conquest was not one concerned primarily with the plunder of our resources – we had few except bogs, mountains and woods, but with the much more important and far reaching conviction that, for Britain, *the conquest and holding of Ireland was an absolute military necessity.*

It is of enormous importance that this political principle be grasped and understood. The history of Ireland over the past four hundred years can only be properly interpreted in the light of this fundamental principle which is as relevant as ever today. The British do not really care a fig for Catholics, Protestants, Unionists, Nationalists, religion or culture, or majority rule – these are all elements in the consolidation of her military aims – that Irishmen fight and kill each other daily in one part of Ireland leaves her unconcerned. Only the military exigencies of the day cause her anxiety, because on these her very survival depends.

Over the centuries England tried, by constant wars and diplomacy, to dominate and conquer Europe. In this she failed – and many European countries remained a silent and, at times, surly, threat to her eastern flank. She met this threat by skilfully setting these countries fighting each other, and in this way gave herself a fragile balance of power. At different times she fought on different sides, all depending where her interests of the moment lay. If one looks back over the history of Europe the hand of Britain can be seen somewhere in every war – and she did not come out the loser.

Things were different, however, on her western flank. The small island of Ireland, where she already had a foothold, was there, and if this little island were ever to become really strong and powerful it could pose, not only to English expansion, but to the very life of England herself, a serious threat. And so Ireland, as a *sine qua non,* had to be crushed and occupied, which in practical terms meant the destruction of Ireland's separate identity, her language and culture, and her reduction, in economic terms, to a state of serfdom, so as to ensure that she could never emerge in any way as a serious threat.

Again and again over the succeeding centuries the wisdom of

this policy became abundantly clear. One very practical example is seen in the Napoleonic wars in the early nineteenth century. If Britain had neglected to conquer Ireland, she would then have had on her western flank a strong nation of probably ten million people, with its own army and its own powerful navy command-ing the surrounding seas. On her eastern flank she would have had Napoleon's superb armies eager and ready to deal a death blow. Trapped between two powerful enemies who could have starved her to death or defeated her militarily on land and sea, she would have had little hope of survival, let alone of becoming a world power.

One does not have to speculate too much to understand what her predicament would have been in the First World War and indeed the Second World War. There is no way she can ever allow a strong independent Ireland on her western flank. The most her generals can accept is a weak, divided nation, in which a substantial portion of the population, both North and South, are willing to do her bidding.

Winston Churchill was in no doubt about these realities when he wrote that the relationships between Ireland and Britain *were established during the centuries when the independence of a hostile Ireland would have menaced the life of England.*

The military suppression of Ireland began in real earnest after the Reformation when Britain began to expand as a world power. A new religion added an extra weapon to Britain's armoury. With untamed savagery millions of Irish people were driven from their lands and replaced by Englishmen. There is scarcely an Irishman or Irishwoman living today of whom it could not be said that an ancestor did not suffer death in this holocaust. Ken Livingstone, Chairman of the Greater London Council, said that the British treatment of the Irish was worse than the German treatment of the Jews.

In one year alone Cromwell slaughtered 600,000 Irish, that is 50,000 per month. This exceeds the reputed world record of Stalin who, in the late 1930s was said to have executed 40,000 per month. By the end of the eighteenth century Ireland was seemingly broken but to copper-fasten her conquest and put the final nail in Ireland's coffin, Britain utilised the potato famine to send some one million Irish to their deaths and another two million to the coffin ships, and in this way halved her population.

These figures may well be somewhat conservative since many historians now believe that the census was not very accurate and that the population was much larger than estimated. If this is correct the number of deaths would, of course, be much larger. Nassau Senior, a British government adviser on economic affairs, said that he feared the famine would not kill more than a million Irish and that would scarcely be enough to do much good. Senior's attitude expressed fairly accurately British political thinking of the day.

In an important interview with Tom McGrath in the *Sunday Press* the world-renowned English historian Professor A. J. P. Taylor, author of twenty-eight books, said that at the time of the great famine Ireland was like a death camp. 'I'm perfectly clear,' he told Mr McGrath, 'that the underlying policy and structure of planning was manufactured by the British and that it was a form of genocide.'

When we rightly condemn the Nazis for their horrendous slaughter of innocent people we should recall that it ended after ten years but the British campaign in Ireland has lasted hundreds of years, and no Nuremberg Trials have yet taken place.

An important element in this conquest was the destruction of the Irish language. This was important for two very practical reasons. Firstly, the British surmised, when a people's language goes their soul goes with it. A people who express their deepest thoughts and emotions for thousands of years through a particular mode and suddenly find this mode destroyed must surely suffer some kind of psychological disorientation which could make them more amenable to conquest. Secondly, by making English the language of Ireland the propaganda war became simpler. English was used in the courts, local authorities, the professions, the civil service, the churches, and most important of all, in newspapers and books.

All children were forced to learn English in the schools, whether or not they could speak it or whether or not it was the language of the home. On the walls of the Irish national schools in later years one could read posters with the following verse:

> I thank the goodness and the grace
> Which on my youth have smiled,
> To make me in these Christian days
> A happy English child.

By the time the Twenty-six Counties were given a measure of freedom in 1921, the Irish language was almost destroyed. It was left to a native Fine Gael Coalition government to give it the final stab in the back by making it a non-essential subject in the educational curriculum and imposing upon the Irish people the eternal shame of knowing that we are the only country in the world where competence in one's native language is not mandatory. It is interesting to note that when Fianna Fáil, under Jack Lynch, got back into power they did not reverse this decision. This, observers say, was one of the early indications that Fianna Fáil was abandoning one of the aims for which it was founded.

In 1921, tired of constant uprisings, and with one eye on world opinion, Britain gave Twenty-six out of the Thirty-two Counties some degree of physical freedom while holding on to economic, cultural, and what one might term, psychological control. This latter was important because it was to continue producing a crop of Irishmen in all walks of life who were ready and willing to promote British interests and the British viewpoint in Ireland.

To ensure that Ireland would remain permanently divided and never pose a real military threat, Britain partitioned the country into North and South. In the North she maintained her physical presence in an old colonial type state. Here she cleverly split the people into two factions giving one faction sufficient dominance and power to control the other and keep them in a state of subjection bordering on a form of slavery. Students of *realpolitik* suggest that she gave the Unionists only marginal dominance over the Nationalists so that they could never feel too secure and would therefore keep suppressing the Nationalists in case the latter might ever increase their numbers to an unacceptable level. The same opinions also state that one of Britain's greatest fears today is that the Unionists and Nationalists would unite – and this they say, she must prevent at all costs since a concerted united effort against occupation could play havoc with her military interests.

A little known cabinet memo of 1949 leaves one in no doubt as to what Britain's intentions are regarding Northern Ireland:

> Now that Éire will shortly cease to owe any allegiance to the Crown it has become a matter of first-class strategic importance to this

country that the North should continue to form part of His Majesty's dominions. So far as can be foreseen, it will never be to Great Britain's advantage that Northern Ireland should form part of a territory outside His Majesty's jurisdiction. Indeed it seems unlikely that Great Britain would ever be able to agree to this *even if the people of Northern Ireland desired it.* (Italics mine)

This memo would seem to give credibility to the thinking that the Unionist aspirations have little to do with Britain's intention of holding on to the Six Counties. No British leader has ever stated categorically that if a majority in the North favoured a united Ireland the British would leave, lock, stock and barrel. What they have said is that there will be no constitutional change without the consent of the majority. This is a negative statement capable of a variety of interpretations. Why did they not say 'the moment there is a majority in favour of a united Ireland, we will leave the country completely and without any conditions'? But they have not said that.

Margaret Thatcher said, after her meeting with Garret FitzGerald in November 1981, that she would support legislation for a constitutional change 'if it were expressed as a result of a poll conducted in accordance with the Act'. This again is a double-meaning statement because the word 'support' gives no guarantee that such legislation would be passed. The Irish people should not forget the bitter lesson of the Home Rule Bill of 1912 which, although almost everyone supported it and it was passed by both houses of parliament in London, it was never given effect. As George Santayana wisely said: 'Those who do not remember the past are compelled to repeat it.'

Britain has very successfully deluded Irish governments into believing that she wants to solve the partition problem when she really does not, for to do so would be too great a military risk. What she wants is to hold on to the North with the least amount of expense. She has brilliantly persuaded us to spend two hundred and fifty million pounds annually in military, police and civil aid to ensure that partition will not come to an end. In that figure I have included not only security forces, but prisons, courts, legal costs, etc.

It is rather difficult to imagine Spain doing likewise to ensure that the British hold Gibraltar, or West Germany to ensure that the Russians hold on to East Germany. Nowhere in the world, except Ireland, does a country protect with her army, police and courts the interests of the invader in those territories which the invader has forcibly occupied. One has to admire, however, the skill with which the wool has been pulled over the eyes of the Irish people, who have to put their hands in their pockets to pay Britain's bill.

This strategic importance of the Six Counties, and indeed of the Republic itself, has been intensified by the new Russian missiles, which can be zoned on to any target with absolute accuracy and can explode a nuclear warhead more than ten times the power of the Hiroshima and Nagasaki bombs. Such missiles launched from submarines two hundred miles off the west coast of Ireland, could obliterate most British cities in a matter of minutes. However, with a sufficient number of tracking stations on the south, west and north coasts of Ireland these missiles could be detected and destroyed in time.

Most political thinkers now believe that British diplomacy is centred on bringing all Ireland into the British defence system without giving up Northern Ireland. Even as far back as 1951 Lord Rugby, the British ambassador to Ireland, told Mr Seán MacBride that Irish harbours would be vital to British defence plans. He also emphasised how necessary the Belfast shipbuilding yard would be to those same defence plans. Although much of the practical elements of what was viable in those days is obsolete, the principle behind the thinking is the same. She still wants our facilities to protect her own people. What happens to us in the process is a matter of indifference to her. The fact is that, if we agree to tracking stations, they will become the first Russian targets and a quarter of a million bodies of dead Irish men, women and children will litter our towns and cities in the first few days of any future war. That is where 'good Anglo-Irish relations' today could lead. Here may I recommend Patrick Comerford's book: *Do You Want to Die for NATO?*

The remarks of two senior British politicians would seem to remove any doubt of Britain's intentions. Mr Humphrey Atkins, a former Secretary of State for Northern Ireland has said:

> Sixty years ago Britain and Ireland – a lot of Ireland – got separated. *I think we can reverse that.* (italics mine)

Again his assistant Mr Michael Mates said:

> It would be important for us, for the two nations, to sing with one voice over defence. *The strategic importance of the island cannot be over-estimated.* (italics mine)

The arrogance of these two statements surely takes some beating. Not only do the British forcibly occupy six of our counties, but they now want to exercise effective control of the rest of the country, not indeed for the benefit of the people of Ireland, but for the safety of British cities.

To do this, of course, she must firstly crush all Republican and Nationalist opposition in the North, no matter what degree of brutality has to be used; and secondly, she must do all in her power to ensure a pliable co-operative government in the South. The many problems besetting us today can, I suggest, be understood only in this context.

To ease the promulgation of this policy, it would be of incalculable help to have in Ireland a government sympathetic to her wishes and a government leader compliant, conformable and generally responsive to her policies. She believes that while Fine Gael and Labour are in power, she can count on such co-operation. While British politicians will admit privately that it should be possible to find also within the ranks of Fianna Fáil the kind of leader they would like, they are quite certain Haughey is not their man, just as De Valera was not their man in the Second World War. Indeed when De Valera formed his first government in 1932, the British Secret Service sent over two top men to liaise with the leaders of Fine Gael (then Cumann na nGaedheal) as to how best to defeat him. One can only wonder if any gentlemen of similar occupation were sent across the Irish Sea when Haughey was elected leader of Fianna Fáil?

As part of her military strategy it is only common sense that she should try to destroy any Irish political party or political leader whom she does not think will act with her interests in mind; but her great genius is that she is able to persuade or influence sections of the Irish themselves to help her do this.

This brings us to the second important question: *How do the British go about transforming the mind of a partly hostile country*

to her point of view? An entire book would be needed to cover
that subject adequately, and we are lucky that such a book exists
and I cannot recommend it too strongly. It is called *British
Intelligence and Covert Action* by Jonathan Bloch and Patrick
Fitzgerald. Commenting on this work, ex-CIA agent Philip Agee
says:

> No thoughtful reader should expect satisfaction or amusement
> from this book. It is a tale of terror, murder, bribery, cheating,
> lying and torture, which have been practised in varying combina-
> tions from Malaya in the early 1950s to Ireland in the 1980s. In
> between, as colony after colony became independent, the British
> security services were trying to install local regimes that would
> protect the interests of British companies. . . The authors have
> brought together an excellent historical survey of secret British
> operations in the Far East, Middle and Near East, Africa and
> Europe over the past thirty years. Their sources are well
> documented and extremely broad. . .

While the British approach differs slightly from country to
country, it follows a broad general design based on their experi-
ences in the past. The entire operation is carefully planned by
MI6 at their headquarters in Century House, Lambeth, London,
where they have a staff of over six hundred and a reputed annual
budget of five hundred million pounds. In this building there is
a special Irish department with a generous budget. I have been
unable to ascertain the numbers or amounts involved.

The first powerful weapon they use in converting a nation to
their point of view – and this may surprise some – is *Flattery*. It
is wrong to think of the British only in terms of torture and
murder. These are reserved for the more unyielding type of
native such as she ran up against in the Anglo-Irish war and in
Northern Ireland today. Unfortunately, as yet, there has been
no published study of Flattery as a British weapon which has
been used with astonishing success in all countries in the past.
The history of Ireland bristles with examples of men and women
who were successfuly bought off by Flattery and Honours.

Flattery is normally directed at the politicians, at the media
and at the civil service, university staffs, the judiciary and personnel of other public institutions.

In the case of politicians the campaign begins by inviting a chosen number to dinner parties, at first in expensive hotels and restaurants and later at the embassy itself. Very often these politicians are introduced to some titled gentleman, a lord, a duke or an earl, who, while more than likely despising them secretly, feigns to treat them as somebody. At such convivial repasts no attempts are made to argue or to put forward a point of view. The approach is 'softly, softly'. The general line put forward by the British is: 'Yes, of course, we freely admit England did you a lot of injustice in the past, but that is over now so let's bury the hatchet and be friends. Only by co-operating and working together can both countries make progress.' At the appropriate moment the injection comes – ever so gently: 'Of course I do not wish to be offensive or speak out of turn but I know that I can say in confidence to you that such co-operation would be difficult with that "chappie" Haughey around.' The words are carefully chosen: 'chappie' is intended to denigrate, yet not to offend too much. Everything would be put politely and courteously but, repeated often enough, its effect could be powerful.

It is not hard to imagine how many Irish politicians – and indeed many members of Fianna Fáil – could fall for this applesauce. Many of them were the sons of small farmers, businessmen and shopkeepers and had never been honoured by anyone higher than the parish priest before. If any mention of Northern Ireland came into the conversation this would be parried by one of Britian's greatest propaganda lies: 'Well, don't you see we must be civilised and settle that question in God's good time with the democratic consent of the majority.'

How effective this line was may be judged by its success even on older erstwhile fighters against the British. Field Marshal Smuts is perhaps the outstanding example. Here at home W. T. Cosgrave, Kevin O'Higgins, Desmond FitzGerald, and many of the founders of the state were subjected to massive doses and soon found themselves thinking like the British themselves. It is, of course, the end result, however it was brought about, that counts. Here in Ireland it was particularly sad to find old freedom fighters, like Frank Aiken and Seán MacEntee, ending their days very close to the British view on Charles Haughey and on the Northern Ireland problem.

Time and again I have listened in amazement to Irish politicians trotting out arguments about British sincerity in building a new future together in friendship – old clichés which I knew were whispered into their ears at some embassy dinner when their brains were befuddled by the best Scotch whisky. Many of them really believed all this and when I reminded them of George Santayana's dictum that 'those who forget the past are compelled to repeat it', they asked me with a shocked expression 'who he was and if I were trained in Moscow'.

There are, of course, those who would say that the effectiveness of Flattery in political affairs is a lot of rubbish and that politicians are not so easily fooled. Before passing judgment, however, they should read the biographies of various world politicians and men concerned with affairs of state. Here they will find hundreds of examples and here too they will learn that few nations in the world are as adept at putting it to maximum use as are the British. Unfortunately politicians read far too little of such relevant material.

A second important weapon used by the British in moulding the thinking of a people and putting their minds into a state of mental twilight is *Control of the Media.*

Anyone who studies the British propaganda operation in Ireland from 1970 to the present day cannot but be lost in admiration for the brilliant way in which it was executed. In a few short years they won over large sections of the Irish population to the British point of view. More brilliant still was the fact that a lot of this work was done for them by Irishmen, who seemingly put what talents they had at the disposal of their hereditary enemy. What a stroke of genius this really was is best seen if one poses the question: How many educated Spaniards would promote the British cause on Gibraltar? How many educated West Germans would promote the cause of the brutal regime in East Germany? It is in the light of these questions that one can judge the incredible success of the British effort in Southern Ireland.

Of course, they never really succeed in getting substantial control of the media because there are always some strong independent journalists and presenters who are dedicated to truth and cannot be very easily influenced. It is to this kind of journalist I have dedicated this book.

Nevertheless by careful planning and prudent, skilful manipulation, they can achieve a considerable measure of success in influencing large sections of the media without the media being really aware of how they are being exploited. The track record of the British in manipulating the media in those countries which she regards as her vassals has been superb. One can read with acute interest in the *British Handbook of Counter Revolutionary Operations* their advice that *manipulation* of the media is much more effective than censoring it.

She cultivates with great persistance and diligence those media men and women likely to be influenced into promoting her ideas – in much the same way as the admen and PR men operate in commercial firms. Here again Flattery plays a major role. It has been said with great truth that scarcely any journalists are susceptible to bribes but quite a few are susceptible to Flattery.

The tactics used to win over the media are very similar to those employed in changing the minds of politicians, with one important difference: they place far more emphasis on winning over the media. The politicians they would see as *reacting* to the pulse of the public whereas the media would *influence* it. The strongest thrust of these efforts would be, therefore, directed and centred on the media.

This usually begins by sending to selected media people invitations to social functions, parties and dinners, where with true British hospitality the champagne, whisky and brandy will be in plentiful supply. The recipients of these invitations are highly flattered and in these informal circumstances and congenial surroundings it is reckoned not to be too difficult to plant the right stories in the befuddled, unsuspecting minds of the media guests. It is said that attached to the British embassy in Dublin there are a number of officials – probably belonging to MI6, though this is not certain – whose main job is to wine, dine and entertain anyone who can be of use to them in presenting the British point of view; to win their confidence and to plant the right stories in their minds. In 1868 Dublin Castle spent £3,000 on this special media entertainment. In today's figures that cannot be far off a quarter of a million pounds. It is said that some of the most shameless and preposterous lies concerning Charles Haughey's private life originated at these parties. Not only that, but these identical stories were circulated at the same time through British embassies in foreign countries.

For some specially selected people, who show promise of

strong anti-Republicanism, there are banquets in the sumptuous surroundings of the embassy itself. Here it is suspected the really strong propaganda surfaces in the form of a kind of subliminal briefing, unknown perhaps to the victims themselves. Here one might hear echoes of Winston Churchill's famous statement that: 'Truth is so precious it must be surrounded by a bodyguard of lies.'

One British commentator who, for obvious reasons must remain nameless, observed: 'If we can get our guests to say to themselves on leaving – "Well, after all the British are a decent lot, they are doing their best in Northern Ireland and we must try to help them, or at least not do anything to hinder them" – then we will regard our work as highly successful.'

The practical result of this mild brainwashing may well be that a journalist could be very reluctant to write or publish a story offensive to such congenial hosts. I do not, of course, suggest that everyone who attends an embassy party comes away brainwashed.

Another powerful weapon in this control of the media is the planting of pro-British news stories and distorted truths on unsuspecting editors. This is usually carried out with extraordinary skill in so far as it is so well concealed that it is not recognised for what it really is and its real source is disguised in such a way that it appears to have the seal of impartiality. A hard pressed editor or sub-editor would immediately suspect a news release from a British press office but his suspicions may not be aroused if the story came from a news agency or news service. What he may not know is that the British own, or have a controlling interest in a lot of news services. In others they have planted their agents who endeavour to ensure that all the news emanating from that agency is suitably coloured.

The British Secret Service have found many other devices extremely helpful. One is to get a British journalist to write an article or a news story for a British newspaper. Selected Irish journalists are then telephoned and alerted to the fact that this important article is about to appear. Very often a precis of the article appears later in the Irish newspaper without either the journalist or the public being aware that the article was virtually without truth and that it originated with MI6.

The recruitment of freelance journalists is another stratagem put to frequent use. The offer made to these people is that they will be paid a substantial retainer, away above the going trade union rate, conditional on their writing articles with an anti-Republican and pro-British point of view. Of course, it will not be put as crudely as that. The usual approach is a link up with some high sounding motive: 'We know you are very deeply committed to ideals of peace and we like to have journalists of your calibre on our side helping us in the promotion of peace, etc. etc.' It is easy to understand how an impecunious freelance journalist might be tempted by such attractive offers.

One intriguing fact about the skill of the British is the use they make of the word 'peace'. Any organisation with that word in its name and concerned with the Anglo-Irish relations can be sure of their full co-operation if required – a co-operation which, of course, is just exploitation. By being associated with 'peaceful objects' the British are able to divert attention from their own use of violence. On the other hand, any organisation with the word 'justice' in its name is anathema to them and they will do all in their power to label organisations seeking justice as subversive or terrorist.

Another artifice in the repertoire is the use made of 'Letters to the Editor' columns in the newspapers. The British see it as a matter of major importance that the anti-Irish and pro-British viewpoint be strongly represented in these columns for the very good reason that they are widely read. While in the main these letters are genuine quite a number could easily be 'plants'. It is by no means unknown that newspaper editors, anxious to contact the writers, have found that such persons did not exist and that the addresses were fictitious.

The distinguished French author and journalist Roger Faligot has the following to say of this effort:

> Army publicity services have been used to inundate newspapers with letters signed 'A Derry Mother of Six'. In 1970, at the beginning of the present campaign, such letters manifested an absence of the Nationalist psychology to the extent that even pro-British editors preferred not to publish them for fear of laying themselves open to ridicule.

An adjunct to this is the writing of letters of complaint about anti-

British television and radio programmes. The thinking behind this is that programme makers are influenced by the letters they get from the audiences. A few score letters of protest, say about Irish nationalistic songs, could have a profound effect on what songs would be allowed on radio and television in the future.

What is termed in Secret Service language as 'grey promotion' is the rather crafty scheme of trying to influence people of importance and standing in the community, such as judges, senior army and police officers, civil servants, leaders of industry, church leaders and intellectual, academic and educational personnel. Very special attention is given to the latter since they are likely to have a strong influence on young students. In his standard work *Falsehood in War Time* Arthur Ponsonby MP (later Lord Ponsonby) has this to say about some of these:

> They were able to clothe the rough tissue of falsehood with phrases of literary merit and passages of eloquence better than the statesmen. Sometimes by expressions of spurious impartiality, at other times by rhetorical indignation, they could by their literary skill give this or that lie the stamp of indubitably authenticity, even without the shadow of a proof, or incidentally refer to it as an accepted fact.

The use of lords and other titled people to impress and influence members of the judiciary is one of the very special techniques of MI6. Some judges whom it would be important to influence may be invited to meet informally – usually for a meal – a titled member of the British legal profession. The conversation will gradually turn on legal matters. No specific cases will be mentioned; it will be just a general discussion and exchange of views but the British point of view will be subtly injected as representing civilised, enlightened legal thinking. Indeed there are those who go so far as to say that specialists with a knowledge of persuasive psychology are called in to advise on the influencing of the legal profession. That is because legal minds are usually sharper than ordinary mortals and more likely to see through attempts at brainwashing. But they never give up. There is no stone left unturned, no outlet unexplored in the fight to capture the mind of a nation.

How the British have captured the minds of their own people

in relation to Ireland is a perfect example of a masterpiece of exploitation and manipulation. For those interested I would recommend reading *Ireland and the Propaganda War* by Liz Curtis. Although this concerns the media only, it is a damning indictment of their servility and shows how the full facts of Britain's role have been concealed, how the government uses newspapers, radio and television to suppress the news and consistently mislead the public about what is really happening in Northern Ireland. To suggest that some similiar techniques are not being used in Southern Ireland would be simply naïve. How much of it goes on here is, of course, unknown. I do not want to give the silly impression that the Irish are queueing up at the British embassy to be brainwashed. But the possibility of quite a lot of it happening here cannot be ignored when we look at the result.

In a matter of little more than ten years the task of moulding Irish opinion to see things from the British point of view was reasonably successful. In the eyes of a large number of Irish people the Northern Nationalists are now thugs, gangsters and criminals, the RUC are men of honour and integrity, the British army, acting in the noblest tradition, are performing the difficult and thankless task of keeping the peace, and the very highest standards of international justice prevail in the courts – as well, those Southern politicians who stand up to the British are seen by large numbers of Irish as undesirable and untrustworthy. This is a remarkable achievement in such a short space of time. But what raises it to the level of genius is that the British successfully used the Irish themselves to do a lot of the work for them – some wittingly, but the majority unwittingly and what copperfastens it for the British is that even if these Irish found out now that they were 'conned' they would find it extremely difficult to go back on what they said or wrote while at the same time retaining credibility.

The two questions which I posed in this chapter are critical to any understanding of the campaign against Charles Haughey. Most important, however, is that we have a clear grasp of Britain's war aims, which include *all* Ireland as her main outer line of defence. Any Irish politician who gets in the way of those war aims should not hope to be handled with kid gloves – as Charles Haughey and Seán Doherty know to their cost. Truth, however, has a strange habit of winning the last battle.

2. Paddies lie down. . .

If the world knew all the injustices those Englishmen, proud of their guineas
and their naval power, have scattered over the earth,
there would not be enough insults in human languages to throw in their faces.
                                                            – JULES VERNE

Carson got all he wanted by guts and backbone.
Our men possess neither one nor the other.
                                        – WILLIAM MARTIN MURPHY

Englands largest newspapers allow no occasion to escape them of
treating the Irish as an inferior race – a kind of white negroes.
                                        – GUSTAVE DE MOLINARI

Servitude degrades men, even to making them love it.
                                        – MARQUIS DE VAUVENARGUE

While Britain never had, over the centuries, really let up in her attempts to keep the Irish people in a state of anglo-mental twilight, she redoubled her efforts after the start of the Northern troubles in 1969. Now more than ever a loyal Irish population was necessary. As we have seen the evidence tends to show that these efforts met with a very high degree of success. I recall a senior British officer, slightly in his cups, confiding to me:

> Think of what we have achieved. Ten years ago you burned down our embassy in Dublin and most of your population hated us. Now we have you eating out of our hands and your government doing our bidding.

However, it would be wrong to suggest that flattery and propaganda alone could achieve the extraordinary present day situation where we have virtually become a satellite of England. There were other factors which helped a great deal and it might be no harm to take a look at two of them. The first of these factors is the attitude of the British ruling classes towards the Irish *–overbearing, arrogant and contemptuous;* and secondly the *submissive servile and unctuous nature of much of the Irish mind.*

How do the British see themselves and how do they see others? Particularly how do they see the Irish?

In the days of Hitler the Germans were exhorted to see themselves as the master race, but this was a shaky and uncertain sprouting from insecure minds within the Nazi party – minds so insecure that they had to keep shouting it day in and day out in the hope that by persuading others they might convince themselves. With the British it was entirely different. They not only believed they were the master race – they *knew* it. It is in the light of this fundamental conviction that we must judge their actions. Their God is the Royal family. The real God only comes second even in the philosophy of some of their highest religious leaders. Nevertheless, He is given a seat on the board of directors, since at times it may be useful that He call to order His followers in other parts of the world, or that His universal prestige be seen to be an essential part of Britishness.

The elaborate structure of British society is based on this duality with the real God as junior director to be called upon in cases of necessity. British interests are sacred, and therefore take precedence over every moral code. The unquestioning acceptance of these principles is fundamental and indispensible to anyone wishing to hold any permanent place, however menial, in that powerful section of society known as the ruling class, that is, politicians, civil servants, army and police officers, trade union officials, diplomats, judges, clergy, secret service agents, editors and newspaper owners, company directors and managers. Once total allegiance is given to these principles, then every pursuit, however unethical, degrading and untruthful is permissable.

It is in perfect good taste to slaughter more than three hundred young sailors on the *Belgrano,* to cut the throats of Argentinian prisoners of war as they were captured, to murder children playing on the streets of Belfast with plastic bullets, to litter Northern Ireland with two thousand graves, to slaughter thirteen thousand Kenyans whose only wish was that they might live as free people, to betray every trust, to double-cross friendly nations, to starve millions to death. All such things are permissable and indeed praiseworthy, provided they are carried out by Her Majesty's servants, with Her Majesty's weapons and in Her Majesty's interests. God, the junior director, can usually be counted upon to voice His approval through his consecrated hierarchy.

Like the gaudy trappings of an American funeral parlour the use of the words 'Her Majesty' have an almost magical power to cover up realities. There is no such thing as Long Kesh Concentration Camp – there is only Her Majesty's Maze Prison. There is no such thing as Castlereagh Torture Centre – there is only Her Majesty's Castlereagh Police Barracks. There is no such thing as legalised terrorists whose trade includes murder – there is only Her Majesty's Special Air Service. The list could go on indefinitely. Like the whitened sepulchres of the scriptures, these magical words cover stupendous quantities of human bones.

Unlike the Russians, who keep their ruling classes in order by a crude form of blackmail, and an even cruder form of punishment, the British keep their ruling classes in order by a subtle form of blackmail and an even more subtle system of rewards.

To an intelligent, bemused outsider these rewards are baffling, since they seem to reach the heights of asininity and poppycock. But to the British they are life's most glittering prize. What is indeed intriguing is that these rewards are not even financial. Incredible though it may seem they are nothing more than a place on Her Majesty's Honours List. It is the burning desire of the most menial civil servant to be received by the Queen in Buckingham Palace and to have some visible honour conferred. It is especially important to the wives of such men to be photographed with the Queen and the knowledge that one will henceforth be known as Lady So-and-So or Dame So-and-So. Mature, common-sense Europeans may be tempted to laugh at this nonsense but for the British it is deadly serious. I have known of talented men who have sacrificed every principle of decency and honour throughout their lives in the hope of a knighthood – men who in any other society could have been great reformers, great innovators, but who in Britain suffered everything to serve dubious British interests. Cruelty, brutality, oppression and even murder are no bar to acquiring such honours. On the contrary, such conduct, regarded as depraved in any civilised country, could indeed be an advantage. Provided it served British interests no awkward questions would be asked, and in many cases would receive royal recognition and the approval of Her Majesty.

However block-headed all this may appear to outsiders, it is the very essence of *realpolitik* in Britain. It would be a grave error of judgement to dismiss the power and force of this dangling carrot lightly. If Her Majesty's Honours List were removed from the British scene there would be only a castrated nation left.

These double standards of pious pomposity on the one hand and criminality on the other, did not escape the criticism of one of Ireland's best political commentators – D. P. Moran:

> The English mind is essentially one which justifies the means by the end, though it may be too dull to see it and too self-righteous to suspect it. It is narrow and bigoted by nature, and it is bloated by the fat traditions of success. All people can, to a degree, deceive themselves when it is in their interest to do so; but this dull, prosperous people have a malign genius for it; they can deceive themselves into believing that blind hate for a race is love of mankind; that massacres are the harbingers of the higher civilisation, that liberty of conscience is liberty to think as they think.

If we are to reach any understanding of the whole calumniation of Haughey process, an awareness of this British mentality is essential. It would also be important to take a look, not only at this mentality in itself, but also how this mentality views the Irish people. Fortunately we can illustrate this in their own words – words not too often brought to the attention of the Irish people. The standard was set at the turn of the century by *Punch* magazine's description of the Irish:

> A creature manifestly between the gorilla and the negro is to be met with in some of the lowest districts of London and Liverpool. . . it comes from Ireland, whence it has contrived to migrate; it belongs in fact to a tribe of Irish savages; the lowest species of Irish Yahoo. When conversing with its kind it talks a sort of gibberish. . .

This is, of course, an extreme view of the Irish, but has it changed very much since then? In an article in the London *Times* in September 1977, a well-known journalist wrote:

> There they go still, the Irish 'pathriots' *(sic)* with minds locked and barred, mouths gaping wide to extrude the very last morsel of folly and consumed with a wild terror that sense may one day prevail.

While hundreds of thousands of copies of the *Express* news-papers are sold in Ireland, those who buy them must surely be unaware that in an edition of the *Sunday Express* Sir John Junor disapproved of the Queen Mother because she shook hands with the distinguished Irish actor, Richard Harris. 'I do hope she was wearing gloves,' he said. Earlier in the year a colleague of Junor's gave as his valued opinion on the Irish: '. . .a society populated by squalid, stupid people with no purpose beyond leading violent, brutish lives.'

Bonar Law, once Prime Minister of England, was blunt and straight, without trimmings: 'The Irish are an inferior race.'

Winston Churchill told Augustus John that if he had his way he would exterminate the entire Irish people. This is quite a good example of the British mind on Ireland. When Churchill spoke these words he had just waged a war against Hitler who had tried to exterminate the Jewish race. In Churchill's view the extermination of the Jews was a crime of world magnitude but the extermination of the Irish race was something to be com-mended and to which he would gladly give his blessing.

If one were to study the lives of most British political leaders over the past few hundred years, paying special attention to the decades of this century, one would find almost unanimity in these imperious attitudes, but what is of unusual interest and what really shows the contempt in which the British mind hold us is their attitude towards other countries who, in a particular event, took the same line as the Irish.

Two examples come to mind. In the Second World War Ire-land's neutrality was viciously attacked, indeed almost daily, by British politicians and the British media. We were portrayed as cowards, traitors, shirkers, because we did not send our young men out to die in their hundreds of thousands so that Britain might survive and Russia might occupy half of Europe. At the time the British press conducted a scurrilous campaign against Mr De Valera and Fianna Fáil, matched only by their recent abuse of Mr Haughey, while at the same time they had only words of praise for W. T. Cosgrave and Fine Gael. The same denunciation was not applied to Sweden, Switzerland and Por-tugal who were also neutral. The British treated these nations with courtesy and respect, judging them as equals with the right to decide their own destiny.

Again during the Malvinas/Falklands crisis when Mr Haughey declined to go along with British jingoism, or to condone mass murder, the outcry against him by British politicians and the British media was nothing short of savage and uncivilised. Again no such campaign was conducted against Italy or Austria who took the same stance as Ireland. These two countries were respected by the British as nations entitled to their own view-point. Ireland was not.

This 'God-given right' expresses itself frequently in acts of contempt calculated to show the Irish governments who are the masters and Irish governments usually react as obedient servants. The UDR, composed to a great degree of the hated 'B Specials', have a number of their members awaiting trial for killing Catholics. Five of these were stationed at Drumadd Barracks where not only Margaret Thatcher but Prince Philip visited and praised the work of the regiment. When a feeble protest was made by the Department of Foreign Affairs, the British simply thumbed their nose at us. How dare the Paddies raise their heads and speak above their station in life? One is tempted to speculate what the British media, and indeed the Irish media, would do and say if Charles Haughey or Seán Doherty visited a Republican paramilitary training camp.

In March 1982 at a press conference which Margaret Thatcher gave in Brussels she contemptuously referred to Ireland as 'The Free State', the name Lloyd George gave us sixty years ago. But her real gem of contempt for Irish politicians came in October 1983 when, having met with President Reagan, she gave a press conference in the British embassy at Washington. Some journalist asked if she had discussed the Irish question with the president. She replied she could not remember. Ireland in her eyes was such a mass of dirt that she forgot whether it was mentioned or not and seemingly forgot also the thousands of graves littered across the countryside by her armies.

The list of deliberately calculated insults flung at the Irish, particularly by Thatcher, is almost endless, but what is especially sad and humiliating for every citizen of this country is the acceptance of such insults – acceptance almost with joy – by some of our politicians and certain sections of the media. One would be hard put to find any other country in the world where such boot-licking attitudes persist; attitudes which must surely strengthen the British belief that we are really a nation of coolies led by duds.

Perhaps these attitudes are best summed up by one of Northern Ireland's most enlightened priests – Father Des Wilson – writing in the *Andersonstown News:*

> The English government is strong in Ireland because the Irish are weak. . . every time our masters have called on us to condemn each other, many of us have obeyed. Yes, your honour, colonel, sir, what Irishman do you want me to condemn. . . just show him to me, your honour, and I'll condemn him. I only wish your honour, colonel, sir, that I had a forelock to touch, but if I get down on my knees, sir, will that do. . . I will still do whatever it is you require of me, because I know that you are superior to me in every way. . . you are English and I am Irish, your honour. . .

I do not think there can be much doubt in the mind of any reasonable person that the British still see us as some form of sub-human species, without any rights of an independent people, who should at all times answer to the crack of the Westminster Whip. The attitude, however nauseating, is understandable for two reasons that have to do with the Irish mind and its attitude towards the British.

The first of these reasons is that for hundreds of years we have been crawling at their feet and begging a few crumbs from their table. They were the masters and we were the hewers of wood and drawers of water, forced to tip our forelocks and make obeisance before our betters whenever they came within sight. Perhaps the most extraordinary expression of that servility was contained in the words of Daniel O'Connell's son, John, when he spoke in glowing terms of some Irish peasants who starved to death rather than fail to pay their rent to the landlords. 'I thank God,' he said, 'I live among people who would rather die of hunger than defraud the landlords of their rent.'

Ingrained attitudes like this do not simply change over-night, and it must be quite difficult for the British to acknowledge the fact that we are no longer their servants ever ready to do their bidding, just as it is difficult for some Irish to stand up on their two feet and accept that they are no longer slaves. It may well take another fifty or hundred years before a proper balance will be reached.

Sadder, however, is the second reason why the British view us the way they do. Today large numbers of the Irish simply live out that servile role in their daily lives. The British are still their superiors; we are not *in* the Commonwealth, but we are *of* it. What is particularly interesting is that this menial outlook is to be found more among our ruling classes and our better educated, now cynically referred to as the Dublin 4 set, than among those closer to the heart of the Irish nation.

In his forthcoming book *A Warning to the Irish People* Nobel Peace prize-winner, Seán MacBride, has this to say:

> Every country which has been the subject of foreign domination or colonialism inevitably suffers from some degree of slave mentality. This does not affect the fundamental desire of the Irish people to achieve a united and free Ireland; it does, however, at times make them ambivalent in their attitude. As has been pointed out by C. S. Andrews, this ambivalence or acceptance of the status quo, is more noticeable among our present day ruling classes and academics, than among the ordinary people of the country whose national outlook and traditions are sound. . . Many of our own politicians, academics and media people have become subservient to this 'slave mentality'. . .
>
> Just as aggressive colonialism in Ireland by Britain has bred a 'slave mentality' among a large section of our people, the feeling that Britain has a God-given right to interfere in our affairs is deeply ingrained in the minds of those who populate the inner recesses of the British establishment.

But this fact has had calamitous results for the country in so far as it shows how the British brilliantly exploited, to their inestimable advantage, this fawning approach to major political problems by some of our politicians.

To illustrate this I give here two lists which, I suggest, deserve careful study. The first list shows the far-reaching political demands made on us by the British government since 1969 to protect their own interests. It will be seen that on receipt of each demand our leaders dutiously granted it.

The second list shows demands made by Irish governments on the British during the same period. It will be seen that while we *granted* every demand, the British showed their teeth and *refused* to grant even one of ours. The Paddies had to be kept in their place!

List One: Demands made by the British.

In the period 1969 to 1973 the Fianna Fáil government, under the leadership of Jack Lynch, moved away from the traditional Republican stand on partition as laid down by their founders. They largely adopted the British view of unity by consent, which was a fraud anyway, since the British never had any intention of giving unity by consent or any other way. The story of how that happened does not concern this book. It is told in detail in Kevin Boland's *The Rise and Decline of Fianna Fáil.*

This perplexing decision had some serious and dangerous after-effects. In publicly accepting the fact that the Unionists had a veto on a united Ireland, it was largely responsible for the formation of the Provisional IRA since the Nationalists of the North and the young Republicans of the South lost confidence in the Irish government; it sowed the seeds of a major split in the Fianna Fáil party; but above all it gave the green light to the British to press ahead and demand maximum concessions, since there was virtually no difference between British and Irish policy on the North. Every one of these demands was granted but more brilliant still was the skill with which the British succeeded in getting the Irish taxpayer to pay for them to the tune of £250 millions per annum.

The first of these demands was that *all Republican activities in the South should be seriously curtailed.* This demand was acceded to. In the first three years of the Troubles more than one hundred Republicans were jailed in the Twenty-six Counties. Irish army and garda patrols were mounted along the border to prevent Northern Republicans escaping from the RUC. Having succeeded here they pressed on by demanding still more stringent measures. We yielded to these demands by introducing the *Amendments to the Offences Against the State Act,* which provides for the sentencing of young men engaged in anti-British activities on the word of a senior police officer without any evidence, and one can also be sentenced if one approves of Republican speeches by applause or a nod. More pressure ensued and we followed that up by *The Criminal Juris-diction Act* whereby Republicans could be sentenced for alleged offences committed in the North or in Britain. No such repressive legislation exists in any other European country.

Earlier they demanded the *Suppression of Republican Pro-paganda* and we acceded to this demand by introducing Section 31 of the Broadcasting Act which prohibited interviews on radio and television with members of Sinn Féin, even though elected representatives, and the prohibition of Republican songs on radio and television. While elected Republicans may not be interviewed on RTÉ, members of the British SAS, the RUC and the Castlereagh torturers whom we brought before the Euro-pean Court have full access to our airways.

They next demanded *Access by the RUC to Irish Intelligence.* This demand was acceded to. The RUC have now access to all Irish police computers. This means they have available to them the information the gardaí have on every citizen. There is now a daily exchange of such information. According to a recent article in a Belfast Sunday newspaper

> As part of cross-border exchange plan RUC men are collecting intelligence in the South at a special office inside Garda Head-quarters in Dublin's Phoenix Park. . . A six-strong team of police from Dublin are believed to be on permanent 'special liaison' duties with the RUC although the number of them based at Knock RUC Headquarters is not known. At least three detectives from the Dept. 3 of E Branch, the official name of the Special Branch (Northern) are based in an office on the first floor of the new building in Dublin's Phoenix Park.

It has recently come to light that secret information passed on by the gardaí to the RUC came into the possession of the UVF and was allegedly used by them for extortions and even murder. Is it any wonder so many people refuse to give inform-ation to our gardaí?

Again the British demanded *The Right to fly British Heli-copters across the Border into the Republic,* and this demand was acceded to. British army Puma helicopters – the same ones that roared over the burial of Bobby Sands so that the graveside prayers could not be heard – are now allowed to overfly into

the Republic, land where they like and take off again. The British
code-name for this extraordinary toleration is *Pumas for
Paddies*. These helicopters land almost daily in the Republic.
For example, one British army helicopter landed in a field near
Clones. When the owner informed the occupants that they were
in the Republic, he was told to 'fuck off' as they knew quite well
where they were.

*The Collaboration of Irish Embassies abroad in the fight
against Republicanism,* was demanded and acceded to. The
embassies of Iron Curtain countries must always look over their
shoulders towards the Russian embassy before making any pro-
nouncement. In the same way it seems as if most of the Irish
embassies must look over their shoulders and ascertain what the
British are thinking before taking any action involving the political independence of Ireland. Some recent St Patrick's Day
Parades in New York give ample testimony of how our embassies
toe the British line. Perhaps the greatest result of this was what
has come to be known as the Ottinger Bill affair. The Ottinger
Bill proposed to pass legislation in the USA banning the 36
American companies in Northern Ireland from discriminating
against Catholics and ensuring they follow fair employment
practices. The Irish embassy in Washington tried to *block* the
passage of this and campaigned actively *against* the Bill. A
spokesman for Irish organisations in United States said:

> The Irish embassy is quite simply conspiring with the British
> embassy to cover up anti-Catholic discrimination in Northern Ire-
> land. I call upon the opposition parties and the independents in
> the Dáil to demand that this disgraceful sell out of the Catholics
> in Northern Ireland by the FitzGerald/Spring administration
> ceases.

In most continental countries British lecturers regularly visit
prominent cities and give talks on Northern Ireland, especially
to academic audiences. These lectures are pure, unadulterated
British propaganda with a minimum of truth. Yet there is not
even a whimper from the Irish embassies.

*The Demand that the SAS and RUC be allowed cross the
Border for the Collection of Intelligence* seems to have been
acceded to, at least in the sense that a blind eye is turned on

their activities. Every year there are hundreds of incursions across the border for what purpose can only be guessed at – certainly not to admire the Irish scenery. Some time ago two jeeps carrying British soldiers drove openly through the streets of one town without any interception by the gardaí. The murder of Seamus Ludlow inside the border at Ballymascanlon is believed locally to have been carried out by the SAS who were seen in the area at the time. A few days later when SAS men were caught by the gardaí, there is no evidence to show that any ballistic tests were carried out on their guns to see if they had been used in the murder. In March 1976 an SAS team crossed the border and forcibly abducted Seán McKenna and dragged him across into the Six Counties. Several young Irishmen known to have Republican sympathies have been abducted in the Republic and brought across the border. The bodies of some have never been found. Two questions asked in the Dáil elicited the information that over a period of years there were 1,300 such incursions! These were the ones known to the government. How many were unknown? Of these only three or four were brought before the courts and in all cases only the lightest of fines were imposed.

At the present moment people living along the Republic side of the border have had their houses searched and furniture broken by the British security forces who seem to cross when and where they like without interference from either gardaí or army. Patsy McArdle, a reputable journalist living in Monaghan gives a chilling account of all this in his book *The Secret War*. To set this in its proper context one must ask the question: Would Norway, Finland, West Germany, or Austria allow the KGB to cross their frontiers and harass their citizens when they liked? Would Britain?

Their most brilliant success, however, in which they achieved the seemingly impossible, was the granting of their *Demands for Extradition*. Almost since the foundation of the state the British have sought the extradition of Irish political offenders to stand trial in either the Six Counties or Britain itself. Fierce resistance to this demand was one of the few things both Fianna Fáil and Fine Gael were united on. So strong were they on this point that even German prisoners of war who escaped from prison camps in the Six Counties into the South would not be extradited.

During the 1950s when the IRA were shooting soldiers and police in the North, the Fine Gael Taoiseach, John A. Costello, a distinguished lawyer, was quite clear that any form of extradition was out. He said:

> In order to prevent any further controversy or discussion on this point. . . there can be no question of our handing over either to the British or Six County authorities persons whom they may accuse of armed activities in Britain or the Six Counties.

It is interesting that there is no reference here to 'political' offence, but in 1982 and in 1984 there was a change of opinion.

In 1982 the Supreme Court extradited Dominic McGlinchey to the Six Counties to face trial for the murder of a woman caught in crossfire in an altercation with the security forces. There was virtually no evidence that McGlinchey committed the offence. In 1984 Seamus Shannon was extradited on a murder charge. Again virtually no evidence was produced that Shannon committed the offence. There was some vague suggestion that there might be fingerprint evidence, but it is highly dangerous to rely on evidence of this nature. Recent technological advances suggest that once a person's fingerprint has been taken it can be transferred on to any object. The Chief Justice, Mr T. F. O'Higgins, in giving his judgment in the McGlinchey case said that to claim immunity from extradition one would have to show that the political actions were 'what reasonable civilised people would regard as political activity.'

While I hold Mr Justice O'Higgins and his colleagues in the highest respect and I believe that their decision was based on what they saw as the correct interpretation of the situation, nevertheless they are not infallible. Many serious and responsible people felt that their decision was mistaken and could have very serious consequences. There is a long series of international law cases which indicate that it is the *motivation* of an act, not its inherent nature, or what reasonable people think, which determine whether an act is political or not.

The unease with this decision seems to have stemmed from the fact that there is no legal definition in our constitution of the words 'reasonable civilised people' and the words 'political activity'. One must ask is everyone who disagrees with that decision, and indeed there are many, unreasonable and uncivilised? Surely the lawyers who opposed it cannot be considered unreasonable and uncivilised? Were Pádraic Pearse and Michael Collins unreasonable and uncivilised? Was De Valera and his cabinet who opposed in arms the government of the day unreasonable and uncivilised? Are the rebels in El Salvador, Afganistan and Poland unreasonable and uncivilised? Will the Irish Supreme Court now extradite defectors from Russia and El Salvador? Can Father Niall O'Brien be extradited to the Philippines? It looks as if they can.

Again the words 'political activity' does not seem to be properly defined. Dominic McGlinchey is a prominent member of a political organisation and has devoted his entire adult life to the activities of this organisation both violently and non-violently. It is hard to comprehend how his activities could be classified as non-political. Worse still we now have reports in the press that the RUC have tried to recruit an informer with large cash inducements to give false evidence against McGlinchey. Is this what we use extradition for? In the case of Seamus Shannon, he stated that he was ten miles away when the murder was committed, and no evidence was produced to say he was not. How could one judge his motive if he were not there?

In August 1984 Minister for Foreign Affairs Peter Barry stated that there was no real democracy in Northern Ireland. Why then extradite people to such a state? Should Mr Barry consider resigning from a government which does so?

Is there any difference between the Diplock Courts in Northern Ireland and the Russian Courts? One distinguished writer described the Russian courts by saying 'Everything about them is true except the facts.' Could the same be said of the Diplock Courts? Does the government regard the Northern Ireland courts as the very essence of justice and fairness? Do they disagree with Mr Barry that there is no democracy in Northern Ireland? Surely an examination in depth by the media here would be an enlightening experience for the Irish public. Would these young men have been extradited if Charles Haughey were in power? I doubt it very much. His statement of 11 September 1984 is valid here:

It is necessary on the occasion of the appointment of a new British Secretary of State for Northern Ireland to point out the tragic consequences that follow from the failure of the British government to respond long before now to the Report of the New Ireland Forum. It is only in an entirely changed constitutional structure that a beginning can be made in bringing peace and justice to Northern Ireland. The present political entity has failed. There is no genuine democracy because the most basic attribute of any democratic society, confidence in the institutions of the state and in particular in the impartiality of the courts and the police, has irretrievably broken down.

The Report of the New Ireland Forum underlined the fact that existing structures and practices in Northern Ireland have failed to provide either peace, stability or reconciliation. As pointed out, Nationalists, for the most part, do not identify with the police or security forces. Far from being able to rely in the normal way on the police and the courts for their protection they are subject to constant and widespread harassment and intimidation. Since the Report was published the situation has deteriorated still further. If the Report were being updated this aspect of the Northern situation would have to be greatly accentuated. The brutal and horrifying behaviour of the RUC in West Belfast on 12 August, the revelations in regard to the activities of the security forces in Armagh and the appalling statements made recently by certain Northern judges completely undermine the credibility of the police and the system of administration of justice in Northern Ireland.

In these circumstances, the procedures adopted by the Attorney General in recent months and the attitude of the Supreme Court in extraditing persons to a totally discredited system of justice in Northern Ireland who could have been tried here for the offences involved must be viewed with grave concern. Fianna Fáil reject the recently published statement by the Minister for Justice which suggests that the inalienable right for the Irish people to the unity of their country can be relegated to the status of a claim which might be bartered for temporary political concessions.

These are but a few examples of the demands we so foolishly granted. There must be scores of others of which we know nothing and which will only come to light in the distant future when the state papers become public.

To balance up the picture it might be no harm to look at the other side, namely the demands made by the Irish governments since 1969. 'Demands' is really too strong a word. We do not even seem to have the guts to demand anything. 'Pleas' would be a better word.

List Two: Pleas made by Irish governments since 1969.

Our first plea was to ask that an 'Irish Dimension' in the whole Northern question be recognised. This has not only been refused but refused with contempt. Politicians of both British parties have been adamant in refusing this request. Mrs Thatcher has said that Northern Ireland is as British as her own constituency of Finchley and successive British politicians have loudly and clearly said 'what we have we hold'. The British are in Ireland to stay and we have been told in no uncertain terms that the only 'Irish Dimension' concerns our role as policemen to do what we are told.

When young men were dying on various hunger-strikes in the North, we made desperate pleas that they be *given enough concessions* to enable them to call off the strikes. Again both the Conservative and Labour parties treated these pleas with contempt. As a result ten young men died despite our pleas and we responded by *increasing* help and co-operation for those responsible for these deaths.

We asked for an *end to the gerrymandering of constituencies in the North.* This again was refused. The Nationalist population of Northern Ireland is slightly over forty-two per cent of the whole. Yet in the Westminster parliament they have only two representatives while the others have sixteen. They should have at least eight. The constituencies are so successfully gerrymandered that anything like a fair representation is impossible.

On purely humanitarian grounds we asked to *Transfer Republican prisoners in Britain to Northern Ireland so that their relatives could visit them.* This was also refused. Irish prisoners in England are forced to live under the most appalling conditions. Let us have a look at one example: a young Irish prisoner from County Tipperary has been on the blanket since 1979 and has been put through the most appalling sufferings. He has only one arm and one leg, yet the British refused to let him use his artificial limbs. He is locked up for twenty-four hours a day without exercise, and refused all access to books, radio,

newspapers and writing materials. The walls and ceiling of his
cell are painted white which have the effect of causing sensory
deprivation and his bed was taken away every morning so he
had nowhere to lie down except the floor. Am I being
unreasonable if I say that there is little difference between that
treatment and what he could have expected from the Nazis?

These horrendous conditions are not new for Irishmen in
British prisons – after all poor O'Donovan Rossa was made to
eat his meals off the floor with his hands tied behind his back.
There are scores of Irish prisoners in Britain, some convicted
on the most dubious evidence, suffering under similar appalling
conditions. All requests made by Irish governments to have these
conditions eased have been refused.

Another request made was the *Removal of the ban on flying
the Tricolour in the Six Counties.* This request has been made
several times and in each time refused. Yet the Union Jack may
be flown freely in the Republic.

We also asked the British to *Cease blocking border by-roads.*
They have constantly blown craters in by-roads just north of the
border and as this interferes with cross-border communications
we have pleaded again and again to cease this activity. Each
time they refused. Not only that but they have erected signs
indicating where exactly the border is. This could be said to be
a good thing, except for the fact that in some cases they have put
up the signs some few hundred yards on the Irish side of the
border where it would seem to be tactically advantageous to
them!

We have also asked the British to *Modify the operation of the
Prevention of Terrorism Act.* Not only has this request been
refused but the laws have been strengthened and extended. Each
year some five thousand innocent Irish travellers and
holidaymakers are subjected to insulting interrogations by police
at British airports and harbours. In some cases it has been carried
out with unnecessary viciousness. In other cases Irishmen have
been detained, beaten and assaulted, and then let go. One can
imagine the outcry in the media if each year Irish police arrested
five thousand English visitors to our country and beat some of
them up.

We recently assembled a *Forum* and debated all aspects of
Northern Ireland. While many down here had little belief in

it, and said it was merely repeating John Redmond's Irish Convention of 1917-1918 at which all shades of opinion, except Sinn Féin, gave evidence, nevertheless the report it issued was at least a worthwhile consensus of opinion. We asked the British to examine it seriously but what in fact they did was to sneer at it and dismiss it with contempt. Their general attitude was 'How dare the Paddies speak up?'

Again and again we have pleaded with the British not to use *plastic bullets* to disperse civilian gatherings, especially where there are women and children. Again and again they have rejected our pleas. Since the beginning of the Troubles some sixteen people, including seven innocent school children, have been killed by these bullets, and over one hundred seriously injured – some blinded and others maimed for life. In most cases there was not even the semblence of a riot. These bullets are lethal. But what is of major interest is they were *only used against Nationalists*. They are not usually used against Orange rioters. But what is even worse, their use by the police in Britain is *forbidden,* they are so lethal. When in August 1984 Seán Downes was shot dead at point blank range by the RUC the Irish government pleaded again to cease using plastic bullets. The British response was to authorise the use of much more lethal weapons that could fire more plastic bullets quicker. It seems to be the old story of 'Paddies lie down'.

Again these are but a few of many refused requests. So the extraordinary picture emerges that we have granted everything the British demanded and they have, in turn, given nothing. That we accept this must surely be a damning example of our servile mind. But when we examine all this more closely what can we conclude? Simply, I think, that the British politicians have walked rings around us and have fooled us up to our eyes. In 1969 we capitulated to the British. Fifteen years and 2,500 deaths later we are still capitulating. Our representatives seem to get tongue-tied, bone-jawed and paralysed when negotiating with the British.

I think we can conclude also that our political leaders are no match for them and have shown themselves unable for the responsibilities placed upon them – in other words, unable for their jobs.

Again what is rather striking is the almost complete silence of the media on all these points. It is hard to blame cynics when they say that much of the Irish media consider what happened to Seán Doherty's escort car near Ballybunion as of more national importance than the erosion of our sovereignty and the almost complete domination of our country by British influence. If there is any substance in this then it is a sad day for the Irish people who have a right to look to the media as their watch-dogs, protectors and defenders.

It was necessary for me to sketch in this rather condensed background so that my readers would be spared a stunted, warped and one-sided version of the events of recent years. The British have no intention of leaving Northern Ireland. Not only that but they are anxious to be given free defence facilities in the Republic. In an article in the May 1982 issue of *International Relations,* Vice-Admiral Sir Ian McGough, former Royal Navy Commander for NATO's North Atlantic area, gives much more than a hint as to what would happen in the event of war:

> . . .if Britain should once again find herself at war – and particularly with the Soviet Union – she could not accept a militant left-wing government in Éire with the prospect of military facilities not only denied to Britain, but made available to her enemy.

Am I being offensive if I ask the smoked salmon socialists in the Labour Party to study that quotation?

The structure of any Irish government is of critical importance to Britain. With a Fine Gael dominated Coalition she feels confident Ireland will ultimately yield to her military demands. They have already bent backwards to grant her every wish and when someone opposes them they say such opposition was damaging to 'Anglo-Irish relations', which seems to be the great excuse for failure to stand up to the British.

What is not so well understood is that within Fianna Fáil itself there may be elements quite close to Fine Gael thinking, a kind of Fine Gael caucus – elements who have not the slightest interest in the party's Republican philosophy and tradition – who would also yield to Britain if they saw it to be to their personal political advantage.

Charles Haughey is not one of these. He has placed on record

more than once that only a united, free, Thirty-two County
Ireland can negotiate any military concessions to anyone. He is
therefore seen by the British to be their enemy and not to be
trusted. Margaret Thatcher put it succinctly when she said 'I
knew my instincts about that man were right. I never should
have talked to him in the first place.' A rare compliment not
extended to many Irishmen. Not only do the British distrust him
but they would be happy to see him destroyed, and especially
happy if his fellow countrymen would do the job for them. That
goal was almost achieved, OPERATION BROGUE very nearly
succeeded.

3. The First Shots

The most dangerous of all falsehoods is a slightly distorted truth.
– G. C. LICHTENBERGER

What does not destroy me, makes me stronger.
– NIETZCHE

*Arthur Griffith's ideas were scrapped without mercy
and in their place we had endless and nauseating abuse of De Valera.*
– J. J. WALSH, MINISTER FOR POST AND TELEGRAPHS

In our long and painful history there were a few imaginative and outstanding leaders who were subjected to the full rigours of slander and vilification by the alert British propaganda machine. Amongst these were Daniel O'Connell, Charles Stewart Parnell, Roger Casement, Michael Collins and Eamon de Valera. To this distinguished company, it seems as if we must now add the name of Charles J. Haughey.

One does not have to search too deeply to find the reason. All of these men had one thing in common; they had, to a greater or lesser extent, stood up to the British and in each case they posed a serious threat to British interests in Ireland. Because they did this they were held to have committed an unforgivable offence for which they had to be denigrated and, if possible, driven out of public life.

The attacks on O'Connell were coarse, crude and sordid. The London *Times* called him 'an unredeemed and unredeemable scoundrel', the leader of 'a system of organised ruffianism'. It published the well known verses:

> Scum condensed of Irish bog
> Ruffian, coward, demagogue
> Boundless liar, base detractor,
> Nurse of murders, treasons factor.
> Spout thy filth, effuse thy slime. . .

'How long shall such a wretch as this be tolerated among civilised men,' it shrieked. Here one is reminded of the hysteria of 1982-83: 'How long must Fianna Fáil tolerate Haughey?'

They accused O'Connell of making money out of the Irish people and some papers showed cartoons of him actually eating Irish peasants. Neither was the sex angle overlooked. They spread rumours that O'Connell was the father of scores of illegitimate children and they even persuaded one woman, Eleanor Courtenay, to write a pamphlet claiming O'Connell was the father of her child. Yet the most exhaustive historical research has shown that O'Connell was a faithful, devoted husband and that these stories were pure invention, calculated only to ruin him.

When Parnell threatened British interests in Ireland the British press could scarcely say a good word about him. They slandered him at every opportunity, even going to the extent of using forged documents to try and connect him with crime. They did not forget the sex angle either. At the time virtually every member of the British ruling class had a mistress but only Parnell's affair with Kitty O'Shea made the headlines, and then only when the time was ripe, and they used their ever-faithful servant, Irishman Tim Healy, to smash 'the march of a nation' and split Parnell's party wide open.

The British Foreign Office embarked upon a campaign of vilification against Roger Casement because he supported the cause of Irish Republicanism, supported the revolution against the British and tried to import arms for the revolutionaries. They are now believed to have arranged and supervised the forging of his diaries to prove he was a depraved homosexual. In a trial, the validity of which raises considerable doubt, like the trials of many Irish in Britain today, they sentenced him to death and had this sentence carried out with the utmost haste. In this they had the support of a large section of the Irish media.

Michael Collins they portrayed as a 'criminal gangster' with a 'lust for blood', a murderer whose bloodthirsty activities destroyed all hope of peace for the Irish people. They did not forget the sex aspect either. They spread the rumour that he was having affairs with Hazel Lavery and Moira Llwellyn Davies and that it was they who influenced him to sign the Treaty. These stories had a devastating effect in Ireland and angered Republicans so much that it may well have been a strong contributory factor in starting the Civil War.

Most of us in the upper age bracket remember the vilification of De Valera. Started and fuelled by the British, the old Cumann na nGaedheal pulled no stops. They even got Cardinal Pacelli (later Pius XII) on their side. He told the British minister at the Vatican how much more he preferred Cosgrave to De Valera. At home they screamed that De Valera's hands were 'steeped in blood'. He started the Civil War and asked the people to 'wade knee deep in brothers' blood'. He was a 'scoundrel, a twister, a dishonest man of no principle, a murderer', etc. As I heard the word 'Houdini' being used in connection with Charles Haughey, I remembered a cartoon I saw in my youth showing a huge circus ring in a tent, Seán Lemass standing to one side with a ring-master's whip in his hand, while De Valera did a Houdini act in the centre. The audience were the people of Ireland. Strange how history repeats itself again and again and how similar treatment was applied to Haughey. He too, like De Valera, was Houdini, the great survival trickster. Once more sex was not forgotten. De Valera was the 'illegitimate son of a Lord Chief Justice', his wife was having an affair with Michael Collins. When illegitimacy was a serious stigma in Irish society, De Valera was constrained to rise in Dáil Éireann and give the dates of his parents' marriage and his own birth to refute the falsehoods being circulated about him by the British and by Fine Gael who regularly referred to him as 'that Spanish bastard'.

Even Seán Lemass did not escape. In a revealing interview with Deaglán de Breadún Charles Haughey records that Seán Lemass was one of those who had to endure personal attack and vilification, and the day he was appointed Taoiseach a personal attack was launched against him by James Dillon. 'That's why I'm very cynical when I hear some of the present Fine Gael people trying to convey the impression that they were supporters and admirers even of Lemass,' said Haughey. 'They were not. They decried everything and they vilified him in every way both politically and personally.'

Again the Irish media largely supported this line of vilification but if we look at the other side of the coin we will search in vain for any similar campaign being enacted against Tim Healy, John Redmond, W. T. Cosgrave, Kevin O'Higgins, Liam Cosgrave, Jack Lynch or Garret FitzGerald. Indeed Garret FitzGerald has been more than once referred to as the 'darling of Fleet Street', so adulatory are the press notices he gets there, and in 1982 the London *Times* advised Spanish politicians in relation to Gibraltar, to follow the example of Garret FitzGerald rather than Charles Haughey. I am not drawing any inferences from these facts or suggesting that because a person is praised by the British media there is something wrong with him.

It does seem to me, however, that it is the function of the media to *inform* the Irish public and to put before them *all* aspects of any situation. When, therefore, the vilification of Charles Haughey started they should have drawn public attention to the interesting pattern which was emerging, namely that Haughey shared the wrath of the British with the great Irish leaders of the past, and that OPERATION BROGUE was well under way. To do this would not have prevented them criticising Haughey, while at the same time it would have presented both sides of the picture to the Irish public. Unfortunately for the most part, they did not do so and their failure must surely bring into question their all-round reliability in reporting the whole Haughey saga.

The first salvos against Haughey were fired in Dáil Éireann on his nomination as Taoiseach by none other than Garret FitzGerald himself. Those elements within Fianna Fáil who believed in the Republicanism of its founders had become strongly dissatisfied with the leadership of Jack Lynch and particularly with his Six County policy in which he seemed to have allowed himself to be influenced too much by the British. Many Fianna Fáil deputies were upset by allegations such as were later expressed by American author Kevin Kelley in his book *The Longest War:*

> Whenever the British government – Tory or Labour – really needed the Taoiseach's co-operation, the pliable Lynch could be counted on to take the subservient stance expected of him.

We will, of course, have to await the publication of Mr Lynch's memoirs to get his side of the story.

Lynch, however, had sometime before privately decided to retire so that the effect of this discontent within the party only advanced the date.

At a Fianna Fáil party meeting in December 1979 Charles Haughey was elected leader by forty-four votes to thirty-eight for his opponent George Colley. By any standards this was an outstanding achievement. Nine years previously he had been fired from the cabinet, arrested at his home, brought to the Bridewell Jail and incarcerated like any criminal. His opponent went into the election with everything in his favour and lost. In fairness, however, it should be said here there was no comparison between the two men. Haughey was a man of outstanding ability and had shown this in the various ministries he held. On the other hand, Colley was something of a middle-weight who never really succeeded in consoling himself for what he might have been. He did not have the greatness required for leadership. His pettiness when Haughey extended the hand of friendship to him proved this, as did also his willingness later secretly to help elements outside the party to damage it and its leader. In adversity men show their true nature; Colley's reactions were certainly not such as to inspire confidence in his ability to lead a great party, and here the judgment of those who thought he could must surely come into question.

When Haughey was proposed as Taoiseach in Dáil Éireann Garret FitzGerald launched into a most unchristian attack on the new Taoiseach – an attack reckoned by many as one of the most regrettable ever uttered in Dáil Éireann and made particularly nasty in that Haughey's aged mother was present. Even many hardened journalists in the press gallery were shocked. The attack was largely personal, contained unexplained phrases and sentences: '. . . recognising how much I cannot say, for reasons that all in this house understand.' What did this mean? Later when he tried to backtrack, FitzGerald said he was referring to political matters, but not everyone believed him. He went on to say that Haughey came to the office of Taoiseach 'with flawed pedigree'. 'His motives,' he said, 'can be judged only by God.' The inference here is that Haughey was so debased that no human brain could comprehend it – only God's infinite mind, not even FitzGerald's, who spoke as if he were sitting on the right hand of God, could plumb the depths.

Can one detect here a note of real fear, a note of actual terror? If Colley had been elected Fine Gael would have been delighted, since under Colley's leadership they could well have decimated

Fianna Fáil at the next election. But Haughey was a different kettle of fish. He was a man of far greater ability than FitzGerald, far closer to the Irish people and a Republican to boot. He had the skill to decimate Fine Gael and the handlers knew it. Would it be presumptuous to harbour the suspicion that all this was not too far from FitzGerald's mind? Could this fear be linked up with an incident which supposedly took place some years before? After the Fine Gael insult to President Ó Dalaigh and his subsequent resignation, the name of Jack Lynch was proposed as an agreed candidate. Political commentators have stated that this idea was turned down within Fine Gael on the suggestion of Garret FitzGerald, the supposed reason being that if Lynch were made President, Haughey would become leader of Fianna Fáil.

If Haughey is so worthless surely Fine Gael should be most anxious to have a worthless leader in Fianna Fáil? There is something here that does not quite add up.

What is also interesting is the reaction of the media. There was not the massive outcry one would expect – the kind of outcry which would certainly have taken place had the roles been reversed and had Seán Doherty or Charlie Haughey made these statements about Garret FitzGerald. Nevertheless not everyone was so muted. *Magill* magazine had this to say:

> Quite the most nauseating spectacle the Dáil has witnessed in decades was the scurrilous and mean attack on the person of Charles Haughey by Garret FitzGerald. In a speech full of moral indignation and self-righteousness the new Taoiseach's character was blackened by a series of innuendo, half-truths and generalisations. . . The pretention to moral self-righteousness is Garret FitzGerald's most salient character defect. . . His performance in the Dáil on Tuesday December 11th demeaned him in the eyes of many who thought him a bigger and more gracious man.

These were strong words and I have not come across any full and effective refutation of them by Garret FitzGerald or by the handlers.

Nevertheless the first shots were fired, and while it would be absurd to suggest that FitzGerald had anything to do with OPERATION BROGUE, the British were naturally delighted.

It was an unexpected bonanza for them and Fleet Street had a field day. Here in Ireland, while all right-thinking people, even within Fine Gael, were disgusted, it set the tone for much of what was to follow, particularly the new Fine Gael strategy in the three elections which took place in 1981 and 1982. In these elections the anti-Haughey venom reached truly amazing proportions, increasing with each election.

After the shattering defeat of Fine Gael in the 1980 Donegal by-election party morale was at a very low ebb. Over the next few months a series of private meetings took place at which every aspect of the defeat was turned upside down and inside out. As a result of these think-tanks the party came to the conclusion that their best hope of defeating Fianna Fáil would be to concentrate on leadership issues rather than on policy matters. For those who examine it closely Fine Gael policy has remained virtually unchanged since the foundation of the party. It is not a policy that has ever attracted the Irish public. It is far too pro-British, anti-Irish language, brutal and inhuman in security matters, and in the economic field tends to place statistics ahead of people. It seemed to the planners that they could not reverse this policy because to do so might look as if they were adopting Fianna Fáil policy, and they rightly concluded they could not sell it to the Irish people either.

They may also have been conscious of the fact that Fine Gael never won an election on policies. Those few they did win, in part, were won, so to speak, by default. The people wanted a change. But they now had a commodity which they believed they could sell to the people. That commodity was their leader, Garret FitzGerald.

FitzGerald was young, modern, trendy, intellectual, spoke of liberalism, pluralism and of breaking with the old traditions, of bringing fresh air into politics, of leading us to a new and more honest Ireland. His life style was impeccable. He was regularly seen in public looking after and attending to his wife. Here was something which could be sold to the Irish public who above all wanted somebody they believed they could trust. The whiz kids and handlers of Fine Gael got together a package, based on the idea of trust, quietly dropping awkward policies and past disasters. 'Trust Garret and therefore you can trust Garret's team.' Even though the success of this campaign was only partial it was

pursued with competence and vigour, and did succeed in project-
ing FitzGerald as the uncanonised patron of Ireland, following
in the footsteps of St Patrick, banishing the snakes. Indeed Fine
Gael always had a leaning towards the supernatural. One of
their early election posters asked people to vote for them because
they were, as they described themselves, 'The Party of Peace,
Plenty and Piety'.

There was, however, another side to the package. It was not
enough to sell a not-wholly-canonised FitzGerald. Satan himself,
in the form of Charlie Haughey, had to be blackened and if
possible driven from political life. Again the awkward question
raises its head. If he were such a bad leader why did Fine Gael
want to destroy him?

Fine Gael's campaign bore a strange resemblance to Nixon's
campaign in 1968. Produce all the personal dirt possible and
throw it and hope that some sticks. Although many decent-
minded Fine Gael members were shocked at these campaigns,
there were others who became numb to the stench of the dirt
they were spewing. None of these campaigns were noted for
idealism, integrity or nobility and they concentrated on falsehoods and innuendoes of a personal nature. While I do not
suggest that Fine Gael worked with the British Secret Service
it can only be a matter of sadness for any Irishman that any
political party in the country should allow itself, however unwittingly, to become an instrument whereby British policy was
vigorously pursued. Fine Gael had previously allowed themselves to be used in this way when they sought to vilify De Valera
in the 1932 and 1933 elections and during the Second World
War. Now it was Haughey's turn.

Most of the Fine Gael and indeed the Labour Party leaders
were careful not to be too closely identified with the campaign
of scurrility. They cautiously distanced themselves in an attitude
of righteousness. The maligning was left to some door-to-door
canvassers who could virtually say what they liked and a lot of
them did. Few punches were pulled. Haughey was depicted as
a crook, a liar, a swindler, a man of no morals, a man whom
nobody could trust, etc. etc. If questions of policy were raised
the answer was ready. Haughey was responsible for all the
unemployment, for the rise in the cost of living, for every evil
that beset the country.

A very special and indeed brilliant technique was used on
Fianna Fáil households. Some canvassers had memorised a carefully compiled list of anti-Haughey members of Fianna Fáil in
the area. When they had recited the litany of his vices the line
then was : 'If you don't believe what we say all you have to do
is to ask Mr A, Mr B or Mr C who are strong supporters of
Fianna Fáil. They will confirm everything we have said.' The
canvassers were, of course, careful not to mention the names of
any pro-Haughey members. I, myself, was approached a few
times with the suggestion: 'If it were not for Haughey, Fianna
Fáil would win the election.' I found out later this was the line
to be played to neutrals. The implication here was : 'Don't vote
Fianna Fáil as long as Haughey is there. You can vote Fianna
Fáil at the next election when he is gone.' All this was subtly
helped on a national level by the song-slogan: *You Can't Have
One Without the Other,* which could be taken to mean, 'You
can't have Fianna Fáil without Haughey and Haughey is a crook,
so don't vote Fianna Fáil.'

Another interesting technique used was to enlist the aid of
ordinary people sympathetic to Fine Gael who were likely to
influence votes. Two particular categories come to mind, i.e.
taxi-drivers and hairdressers. These categories are in the way of
constantly engaging people in conversation and many of them
were used to the full, not in influencing their customers to favour
Fine Gael which would be fair practice, but in casting aspersions
on the character of Charlie Haughey. Similar help was enlisted
from bartenders, shop assistants, etc., not unfortunately, to promote policies, but for character assassination.

A particularly nasty piece of work was the circulation of
unidentified pieces of stencilled papers, by persons unknown,
amongst office and factory workers and indeed private houses.
These were meant to be ironic and funny – but they were anything but harmless. Here is one I have salvaged from several. I
reproduce it exactly as I got it:

> We have the distinguished honour of being part of a committee to
> raise £5m, for placing a statue of Charles Haughey in Dáil Éireann.
> The committee was in a quandary as to where to place the statue.
> It was not thought wise to place it beside the statue of Pádraig Pearse
> who never told a lie; or beside De Valera who never told the truth,

since Haughey could never tell the difference.

We finally decided to place it beside the statue of Christopher Columbus the greatest wheeler-dealer of all times for he left not knowing where he was going; upon arriving he did not know where he was and returning not knowing where he had been.

And did it all on borrowed money.

Over 5,000 years ago Moses told the children of Israel:–

'Pick up your shovels, mount your asses and camels and I will lead you to the Promised Land.' Nearly 5,000 years later Dev said:–

'Lay down your shovels, sit down on your asses, light a camel. . . for this is the Promised Land.' Now Haughey is stealing your shovels, kicking your asses, raising the price of camels and mortgaging the Promised Land.

Haughey's Erection Committee

It is said that Charles Haughey is considering changing the Irish Flag from a tricolour to a condom because it stands for inflation, halts production, promotes a bunch of pricks and gives a false sense of security while being screwed.

What sick mind composed that I do not know. Neither do I know what even sicker mind directed its distribution. If one of the other political parties is responsible then they have every reason to be thoroughly ashamed.

This campaign penetrated almost every home in the country, and while it did not win the election it had a profound psychological effect. It did succeed in vilifying Haughey, but of equal importance, it created a favourable climate or atmosphere for the further and more vicious vilification which was to follow.

Naturally the British were delighted. Once again they looked on with glee at a vast army of Irishmen destroying the man they wanted to destroy. No wonder Fleet Street threw its support behind Fine Gael. It was the De Valera saga of the 1930s repeated all over again. Saddest of all was the fact that a lot of the Irish media acquiesced in this campaign. Again I emphasise that their duty was to put the whole truth before the Irish public, to have analysed in a penetrating way these campaigns, to have shown the public that elections should be fought on policies and not on personal abuse, to have cut through falsehoods and to have alerted the people to what was happening. Unfortunately in this task they failed. By and large the public were given a one-sided view. That Haughey succeeded so well in these elections in face of such bespattering is surely an indication of the hightest qualities of political leadership, as well as an unusual support at grass-root level. Looking at world history one would find it hard to come across any international leader who so successfully defeated, and even humiliated, the vast range of forces against him. No amount of whitewash can refute this fact. Even some of the British recognise this: 'As a politician Haughey is head and shoulders above anyone else in Ireland,' wrote John Cole, the BBC political editor. '. . . He has an inner core of toughness which explains his miraculous durability.'

Even though in the end Haughey won the last battle on the famous 'night of the long knives' in February 1983, the media were remarkably silent on why they had failed so badly in influencing the vote or indeed forecasting the result. Many of them have now learned their lesson, but for some few the abuse of Haughey will sadly remain a life-long crusade. No matter how overwhelming the evidence they are confronted with, they will stick with their errors to the end. That is a great pity. The Irish public deserve better. They deserve to be presented with both sides of the coin so that they can make up their own minds.

4. Onward Christian Soldiers

He who begins by loving Christianity better than Truth will proceed by loving his own sect better than Christianity and end by loving himself better than all.
                                        – SAMUEL TAYLOR COLERIDGE

There is no doubting the good intentions of Garret FitzGerald's government. . . but goodwill is not enough. They have to get their men.
                                        – EDITORIAL: *DAILY MAIL,* November 1983

It may be no harm now to take a look at some of the incidents in Charles Haughey's recent political life which were held up as being in some way reprehensible and see with what justice and fairness these incidents were presented to the public.

1. The Arms Trial

There has been a great deal of nonsense talked about the Arms Trial of 1970, in which Charles Haughey, amongst others, was tried for attempting to import arms illegally. The media went to town on this trial. They portrayed the incidents which gave rise to it as shattering mind-boggling events in the history of Ireland. It was, in fact, nothing of the sort. The Irish public regarded these events with a sort of mild curiosity and were in no way as outraged or shocked as the media seemed to suggest. In fact the majority had a secret sympathy with those on trial and many responsible people openly admitted that, taking into account the brutalities of the RUC and the British army, they themselves would have no hesitation in helping to import arms or indeed supporting the IRA.

This Arms Trial is one of the weapons that has been used down the years to further malign Haughey. But in a strange way it has backfired. While Dublin 4 may have been shocked at the very idea of importing arms to be used against the British, a majority of the Irish public had a sense of understanding with the alleged conspirators.

Magill magazine came to Haughey's defence:

Certainly Haughey's impropriety bears no relation to the magnitude of the accusations that have been flung in his direction over the years. He played no part whatever in the setting up of the Provisional IRA. There is absolutely no evidence that he at any time assisted in the importation of arms for the purpose of 'murdering fellow Irishmen' as is regularly charged. Suggestions that he was guilty of being involved in an attempt to overthrow the state or was guilty of treason are simply outrageous. . . To have suffered the indignity of dismissal from the government for an action which was at least in conformity with government policy at the time was very rough justice. To have been dragged before the courts on charges arising out of this was scandalous.

But a lot of the media did not see it in quite that light and while they highlighted many inaccuracies they chose to ignore a series of very searching questions which were fundamental to any understanding of the Arms Trial.

On 5 May 1970, the leader of the Fine Gael opposition, Liam Cosgrave, went to Jack Lynch, the Fianna Fáil Taoiseach, and said he had information concerning the involvement of government ministers, including Charles Haughey, in an attempt to import arms illegally. Many say that Cosgrave tried to leak this information to the press a week previously but they did not bite.

It was this interview which triggered off the Arms Trial and the dismissal of the ministers. Mr Cosgrave has never disclosed the source of his information, nor have the media ever seriously delved into it. Much as one would like to know where the information came from it must be made clear that Mr Cosgrave has a perfect right not to disclose his source.

Among others, there are two principal sources from which Mr Cosgrave could have got this information. He could have got it from a high-up official in the Department of Justice or in the Gardaí. In either case it was both illegal, unethical and dangerous for any servant of the state to pass on highly sensitive and secret information concerning government policy and government ministers to a member of the opposition party who might well be tempted to use it for party political purposes. In any civilised democratic state an action like this would certainly be grounds for the instant dismissal of the civil servant concerned.

The name of one senior garda officer has been regularly mentioned by what is known as 'informed sources' as the person who gave the information to Mr Cosgrave. This man is now dead and as there is no really solid proof it would be unfair to reveal his identity.

Nevertheless while Mr Cosgrave can be criticised for not disclosing the source of his information in confidence to the Taoiseach, Mr Lynch was seriously remiss in not closing ranks and calling Mr Cosgrave's bluff by refusing to discuss the matter further until the sources of information were disclosed. This would have stopped Cosgrave in his tracks. He could not accuse Lynch of refusing to act and he could not easily disclose his sources. Had Lynch been politically astute enough to out-manoeuvre Cosgrave, the matter most likely would not have gone much further. But it was Cosgrave who out-manoeuvred Lynch, bringing an abortive Arms Trial in which the defendants were acquitted, the government humiliated and a serious split brought about in Fianna Fáil. That is what the Arms Trial achieved. Fine Gael had every reason to be proud of Cosgrave. His was a master political stroke.

Another element never seriously examined by the media was the question of whether the whole thing was set up by the British Secret Service to split Fianna Fáil and that Mr Cosgrave unwittingly helped them. This theory is fairly widely held and it is somewhat surprising the media did not examine it carefully.

The source of Mr Cosgrave's information raises questions fundamental to the security of the state, yet the bulk of the media mostly pursued irrelevancies. If the shoe were on the other foot and Mr Haughey made such disclosures without stating his source would the media have let him off so lightly? Can one detect here the beginning of a pattern? Where events are likely to embarrass Mr Haughey and Republicanism do the media generally investigate and report fully? Where events are likely to embarrass the British or Fine Gael do the media remain silent? Again and again these questions will surface.

2. Telephone Tapping

The Post Office Act of 1908 gives the police power to intercept and open letters as well as to tap telephones and record conversations. The only rule which governs these operations is that they must have the authority of the Minister for Justice. There are no other restrictions. It is important to grasp this fact at the outset. It is true that various ministers have from time to time laid down individual guide-lines, but these are merely what they say, just guide-lines and have no legal effect, and are certainly not binding on any subsequent holder of the office. So that when a Minister for Justice, such as Mr Seán Doherty, or police acting under him, put a tap on telephones they were not acting in any way that could be said to be illegal or indeed improper. Seán Doherty was not in any way bound by the guide-lines laid down by the previous ministers. In fact it seems every minister had his own individual guide-lines.

Another aspect of the telephone tapping that tends to be obscured is the fact that when the police tap someone's telephone this does not mean that they consider that person a criminal. It simply means that others ringing up that person may be suspect. Indeed a senior police officer made that quite clear when he said:

> . . . it has to be accepted that the phones of innocent people not associated with crime or subversion will be tapped. . . You could find out more about crime by tapping the phone of a parish priest than you would from the phone of a criminal.

I myself am reasonably satisfied that, for a time at least, my own personal phone was tapped. This did not mean that the police considered me suspect, but because of the nature of my work as a writer and a publisher many of those who were telephoning me were not exactly the darlings of the gardaí, and consequently the forces of law would very much like to know what these people were saying.

Yet another element in the phone tapping which has been kept somewhat in the shadows is the fact that it has been going on for a very long time and has been accepted by all governments as a legitimate, if distasteful, activity. If a foreigner were to read our newspapers over the last year or two he could be forgiven if he came to the conclusion that Charles Haughey was the inventor of telephone tapping and that Seán Doherty was his chief engineer. Nothing could be further from the truth. *The various Fine Gael dominated Coalitions were, and indeed are, unre-*

mittingly busy in the phone tapping business.

In an article in *Magill* magazine, Frank Doherty, a distinguished journalist with expert knowledge of these affairs, gave lists of those whose phones were believed to have been tapped and the list is frightening. It included journalists, trade union officials, solicitors, senior counsel, priests, bishops, politicians. The list even includes the name of Charles Haughey himself, whose phone, other sources also reveal, was tapped for a considerable time. If anything, Seán Doherty was somewhat of a novice compared to some of the experts of past Fine Gael dominated administrations. However, the most regrettable feature of all this is that the media at large chose to ignore these points and to mislead the Irish public into seeing Seán Doherty as a veritable ogre when, in truth, his participation in this nasty business was minimal.

Seán Doherty was Minister for Justice, holding in his hands complete responsibilty for the security of the state. When it came to his attention that highly secretive and sensitive information was being leaked to the press he became alarmed. This was a matter of the utmost seriousness involving the whole fundamental question of security and if Doherty had not acted at once he would have been guilty of treason.

In *realpolitik* terms this meant that somewhere in the higher echelons of power there was a mole who was passing out information. In Doherty's view no Minister for Jusice could tolerate such a situation. He discussed it fully with senior garda officers and as a result a tap was put on the telephones of certain journalists in the hope of finding out who the mole was. Seán Doherty did not put any pressure on the police to tap the phones of any particular journalists – this was later confirmed by a senior police officer. He did, however, put pressure on them to find the mole. The tapping of these phones had no political overtones whatever and were purely initiated to try and trace the source of the leak, but even if it had political overtones was this so unusual? Surely no one would seriously suggest that Fine Gael would not make use of material originating in telephone taps for political purposes! Moreover, when these taps were put on, Charles Haughey was unaware that this was being done as he was unaware of the names of the journalists in question. Both the minister and police were later at pains to point out that the journalists whose phones were tapped were in no way suspected of any illegal actions. Concerning the general operation the then Garda Commissioner was later to say:

> I am not saying journalists set out to undermine the security of the state but in the pursuit of a major story they may unwittingly do so in disclosing government secrets.

It goes without saying that all security measures, including phone tapping, are highly confidential and insofar as I am aware there has never in the past been a major breach of that principle in this country. Indeed to protect such principles the Official Secrets Act exists and it provides very heavy penalties for those who breach it. However, Section 4 (11) provides:

> A person shall not communicate any official information to any person unless he is duly authorised to do so or does so in the course of and in accordance with his duties as the holder of a public office or when it is his duty in the interest of the state to communicate it.

Governments may come and governments may go but the state secrets remain. In 1932 it must have been a temptation to the new Fianna Fáil government to expose some of the police secrets of their predecessors but they refrained from doing so, as indeed did the Coalition government of 1948.

It was, therefore, a matter of more than ordinary surprise when, early in 1983 after a change of government, Mr Michael Noonan, the Fine Gael Minister for Justice, went on television to confirm reports in a newspapers that the previous Fianna Fáil administration had tapped the phones of two journalists.

This deserves a closer look. What he was saying was that highly confidential and secret government information published in the press was true. No one in the media seems to have referred to the fact that his primary duty was not to confirm or deny what was published, *but to find out who in his department leaked the information.* Since all kinds of articles, some true, some false, regularly appear in newspapers about confidential matters and are usually ignored by ministers, there was no obligation or urgency on Mr Noonan to confirm the tappings. There was, however, a solemn and indeed statutory obligation on him to find out who leaked the information and to have that person brought publicly to justice. The media seemed to have over-looked this important matter. Here was an unprecedented dis-closure of state secrets by a responsible minister. I am presuming that he was legally entitled to do so and had exempted himself from the provisions of the Act but it is hard to see how it was his duty in the interests of the state to merely confirm a news-paper report. But even if he saw it in that light it is strange that he gave the names of two journalists only. In the 'interests of the state' one would have expected him to give the names of all those whose phones were tapped – including those tapped by Fine Gael.

Again the media at large overlooked another deeper impli-cation of this startling event of national importance. But not so former Garda Deputy-Commissioner Ainsworth who said that the Minister for Justice was unwise to breach fundamental state security by the disclosing of official surveillance when he could have told the journalists privately. Mr Ainsworth explained in an interview with the *Sunday Independent:*

> The making public of any phone tap damages the whole security operation. And not only that but in dealing with a security opera-tion or apparatus of any kind one must consider that an enormous number of innocent people become involved. And when their names are mentioned and become public, despite the best efforts there is a shadow cast across them.

Indeed, despite his distinguished record as a public servant, the good name of Mr Ainsworth himself was not to escape those bent on detraction.

While I take the charitable view that Mr Noonan's television disclosures were purely coincidental with an attempt to unseat Mr Haughey as leader of Fianna Fáil, there is another major aspect of this phone tapping business which the media again overlooked. Highly sensitive information was being leaked for some time and Deputy-Commissioner Ainsworth was engaged in an internal garda investigation into who was doing this when a change of government came. The new Fine Gael minister, Mr Michael Noonan, who more than once said that he does not interfere in operational matters, decided to interfere in this investigation. He ordered it to be stopped forthwith, and when Mr Ainsworth appealed against this order without success he was told the matter was 'a source of irritation to the minister'. So, as far as one can judge the mole is still there but why a fundamentally correct investigation of such national importance should irritate the minister certainly needs further explanation.

The extremely unsatisfactory involvement of the Coalition in this affair has prompted Mr Ainsworth to call for a judicial enquiry, not only into the phone tapping, but into political involvement in police affairs over the past ten years. Despite the fact that Dr Michael Woods, the Fianna Fáil spokesman on security, has supported Mr Ainsworth's case, the request for the judicial enquiry has been refused by Fine Gael. Why they have turned this reasonable request down is anybody's guess.

Seán Doherty too has asked for a judicial inquiry and he has very correctly pointed out that he would not be bound by the Official Secrets Act in giving evidence before such an inquiry. He would then be able to tell the whole story of what happened. This does not sound like the action of a man who is trying to cover up something.

On the other hand, one cannot help viewing with suspicion Fine Gael's refusal to hold such an enquiry. Can they be accused of a cover up?

Later when some of the transcripts of the phone tapping were published in the press Garret FitzGerald referred to the contents as 'improperly intercepted' and that there was an 'original offence'. When Mr Ainsworth challenged him to state what the offence was and what law was broken FitzGerald backtracked and said he was speaking 'metaphorically'. Can he complain if eyebrows were raised? Can he complain if people doubt him?

As well as making public the confidential information about the telephone tapping of the two journalists Mr Noonan also made public the contents of a conversation between two Fianna Fáil ministers, Mr Ray MacSharry and Mr Martin O'Donoghue. Surely nothing can be said in favour of this kind of conduct? Is there any one of us who would like our telephone conversations made public? Would Mr Noonan like his telephone communications made public? Here I am reminded of an incident recounted in Kevin Boland's book *Fine Gael – British or Irish?* The day he took over as Minister for Defence from the Fine Gael minister

Seán MacKeown he found in the safe a highly confidential document in the form of a memorandum from the Taoiseach which had been left there by his predecessor. Mr Boland might conceivably have made great political capital out of making this document public, but his conception of correct ministerial behaviour was not to do so and he handed it back to the Secretary of the Department. It does not seem as if Mr Noonan's concept of ministerial behaviour would be in line with that of Mr Boland. Seán Doherty has been criticised for loaning the equipment to Ray MacSharry. It is hard to see how this was improper. As well, Mr Doherty has consistently asked for a judicial inquiry which has not been granted. Such an inquiry would clear up this matter fully.

In all this distasteful affair the bulk of the media seemed obsessed with hammering Seán Doherty for meticulously correct ministerial behaviour, and censuring Charles Haughey who had nothing to do with it at all, so perhaps we should ask a few questions which the media might usefully have asked, but did not – questions which should have been hammered again and again until answers were forthcoming.

Why did Mr Noonan find it necessary to take the unprecedented step of making such highly sensitive material public? Did he go after the mole who was leaking information? If it were a matter of national importance which the public should know why did he not give the names of the journalists whose phones were tapped by Fine Gael? Was it merely a coincidence that at the time of his disclosures there was an attempt being made to split the Fianna Fáil party over the leadership issue? Why did he stop Mr Ainsworth's investigation into the identity of the mole who was passing information, when Mr Ainsworth was hot on his tracks? What steps, if any, has he taken to identify and root out the mole who is apparently still there? Has he any guarantee that the mole will not pass out Fine Gael secrets? What guarantee has he that state secrets will not be passed out to the British, the Russians, the CIA or the SAS? Why have both himself and Garret FitzGerald refused a sworn enquiry into the whole matter?

It may well be that Mr Noonan can provide answers to these questions and, if he can, he would ease a lot of public disquiet by providing them; but if he does not, even at this late hour, the media should consider keeping on his trail until he does.

Another telephone tapping question concerns the bugging of Seamus Mallon's hosts, the Moynas at Kilbarrack. Who did this? Was it a British Secret Service unit working in collaboration with a certain element in the gardaí? In an article in the Belfast *Sunday News* Frank Doherty, a responsible and highly regarded journalist, suggests there was far more to this bugging than meets the eye. He suggests that this affair may well have been a vital cog in OPERATION BROGUE. Mr Doherty says:

> The finding of a hidden microphone bug at the home of Michael and Marjorie Moyna was the start of something big. It led to the discovery that a group of detectives in Dublin Castle's Special Branch were working for Britain's Secret Service (MI5) bugging houses, tapping phones unofficially and following suspects. . . Until the Mallon bugging – although there were some suspicions – the full extent of British intelligence operations in the South were unknown. Now loyal detectives in Dublin Castle have been piecing together the bits of the jig-saw puzzle and they have come up with a startling picture.

This startling picture of which Mr Doherty writes was that the Irish Special Branch had been well penetrated by British spies. Not only that but they succeeded in having our counter-intelligence service purged.

If this is correct it is such an alarming state of affairs that one would hope the media would leave no stone unturned to get to the bottom of it.

One can, however, understand the reluctance of the media to investigate this if an article in *Phoenix* magazine in August 1984 has substance. According to the article a policy decision has been taken by the gardaí to blacklist four journalists and one photographer who have not toed the official garda line in this matter by ceasing to investigate the bugging. They have been constantly probing the matter and are believed to be very close to establishing the identity of who did this bugging. Is it a coincidence that all of these journalists have had visits in their homes from the Special Branch? It would be helpful if Mr Noonan answered that question on his next television appearance. Surely all this should be investigated by an independent judicial inquiry.

3. The Malvinas

The crisis over the Malvinas provided the enemies of Mr
Haughey with another opportunity to vilify him in much the
same way as De Valera was vilified when he asserted Ireland's
right to stand aside and let Britain provide her own cannon
fodder for her wars. The facts, which have been somewhat
crudely distorted, are indeed very simple and straightforward.

Britain was every bit as much an aggressor as the Argentine.
An aspect of the crisis which the media regretfully forgot to
point out was that the British claim to the islands was bogus. In
the nineteenth century she seized and occupied them by sheer
naked aggression. Like the Six Counties, she has since held on
to them by force. Again it was a pity the media did not draw
public attention to the fact that the invasion and occupation of
countries by Britain has come to be regarded as a moral right
which Irishmen are expected to support, even if it is part of their
own country.

The Argentine had tried peaceful means for a long time. They
negotiated with various British governments and year by year
they were given the same contemptuous brush-off that we, here
in Ireland, know so well. Then after twenty years of fruitless
trying they invaded the islands. Britain reacted by sending out
a task force to repel them – in the interests of justice, as Mrs
Thatcher said, and she later explained:

> You have to be prepared to defend the things in which you believe
> and be prepared to use force to secure the future of liberty and
> self-determination.

That quote could easily be inscribed on a plaque and put up
on the wall of Sinn Féin headquarters on the Falls Road. It
would not be necessary to change a syllable.

Michael Foot, at that time leader of the Labour Party, closed
ranks and supported her:

We can hardly forget that thousands of innocent people fighting for their political rights in Argentina are in prison and have been tortured and debased. We cannot forget that fact when our friends and fellow citizens in the Falklands are suffering as they are at the moment.

If we substitute 'British Commonwealth' for Argentina and the 'Six Counties' for the Falklands Dominic McGlinchey might have made the speech.

One very significant point of contrast here shows how magnificently the British united and closed ranks, and how the Irish failed dismally to do so. Virtually all British parties, institutions, media, etc. united behind Thatcher. England was in crisis and they stood shoulder to shoulder together. Ireland was in crisis too. Should she abandon her neutrality, her independence, to help an aggressor who forcibly occupied part of her own country? When Charles Haughey as leader of the nation decided that we should not, there was no standing together shoulder to shoulder as one nation. Many politicians, media and institutions showered abuse on him. It was the old story of Britain always having Irishmen to help her cause, however unwittingly.

While the media in this case were most unhelpful they were even more so when many failed to inform the public that the real reasons why Britain invaded the Malvinas had nothing to do with freedom, self-determination or honour. One reason was the possibility of finding either oil or gas off the islands. Another was the fear that Ronald Reagan's policies in South America might fail and that the whole continent might well develop into a left block. A defence foothold in the area was therefore considered necessary. A third and more sinister reason was that Thatcher was losing popularity and with an election coming up she needed to rouse the old British jingoism, rally-round-the-flag-boys, rule Britannia, etc. etc. It all paid off, however, but at what a cost in human blood and misery and unhappiness and the loneliness of bereavement. Nevertheless, Thatcher, now looking like a Churchillian figure, won her election, and FitzGerald placed on record support for his conception of Anglo-Irish relations, but who will console the heartbroken fathers and mothers, widows and orphaned children, that this totally unnecessary war left behind it?

There are many things in the career of Charles Haughey that one can find fault with but his behaviour in the Malvinas crisis was magnificent, standing head and shoulders above any other leader involved, and was such that any Irishman anywhere in the world could be proud of it.

When sanctions were first asked for he reluctantly agreed because the other EEC countries were applying them. The idea behind these sanctions, however, was to force Argentina to withdraw and to settle the dispute by diplomatic means. When, however, all EEC countries had agreed, Britain without waiting for any indications or results, plumped for the jingoism and sent her army and navy to invade the islands, like an elephant prancing around with diarrhoea. Was Ireland, who had seen that elephant in action so often, to tag along? Haughey was quite clear on the matter: 'We cannot,' he said, 'support sanctions that are themselves in support of military action,' and he withdrew his earlier imposition.

Then came the horrible sinking of the *Belgrano*. She was tracked for thirty hours as she steamed home in neutral waters by a British submarine and was torpedoed without warning in those same neutral waters. It has now been fairly well established that Margaret Thatcher was responsible for this crime – the killing of 368 Argentinian sailors. I seem to recall her own words of the past, 'murder is murder is murder'.

The British media went hysterical in their abuse of Haughey. A lot of the Irish media followed suit. Garret FitzGerald dutifully trotted along behind Thatcher and condemned Haughey for destroying 'Anglo-Irish relations', just as his predecessors in Fine Gael condemned De Valera for destroying 'Anglo-Irish relations' when he refused to hand over our ports and turn the manhood of Ireland into cannon fodder for Britain. Here the media could have helped greatly if they defined for the public what 'Anglo-Irish relations' meant. Are the words a mere cover up for bootlicking and toadyism? Were 'Anglo-Irish relations' destroyed by the 1916 Rising? By the Black-and-Tan War? By the removal of the Oath of Allegiance? By the declaration of a Republic? Did these words mean the mutual respect two free and independent countries had for each other, or did they mean the grovelling of one country on its knees to merit a word of praise or a few crumbs from the table of the other – perhaps a table in the House of Lords? Unfortunately the media did not delve too deeply into the question and the Irish public were left in the dark as to the real issue concerning the Malvinas crisis, and to the use being given to the term 'Anglo-Irish relations'.

They were not, however, left in the dark as regards Haughey's character. He was a betrayer of trust, a destroyer of this puzzling 'Anglo-Irish relations' and an enemy of the Irish people. The similarity with what was being said by the British and Fine Gael about De Valera during the Second World War is extraordinarily close.

I speak of this matter with some personal feeling. I was in the army during the Second World War. Were it not for De Valera's tough and principled action, then, in dumping 'Anglo-Irish relations' I as well as probably 100,000 other Irishmen, would be rotting in foreign graves, and our dependents would have the dubious consolation of knowing that we died defending Britain, and 'Anglo-Irish relations'. This is the *realpolitik* of neutrality.

Some of the statements made following Haughey's decision to withdraw support and after the sinking of the *Belgrano* made interesting reading. Garret FitzGerald said:

> Whether and how time will heal the unnecessary breach with Britain is something we must leave to the future. So also must we leave the final verdict on this episode.

And again in July 1982:

> We have seen him (Haughey) for the most short-term of reasons, in a by-election situation, burning up the path of Anglo-Irish co-operation behind him by his gratuitous anti-British gesture over the Falklands issue.

Mr Austin Deasy, Fine Gael, said:

> The Government's blatant anti-British stance on the Falkland Island issue is disgraceful and is a pandering to the perpetrators of the politics of hate which is so prevalent in elements of our society. . .

Mr Barry Desmond, Labour, said:

It was of critical importance to the future of Anglo-Irish relations that the British Government and British political parties should fully appreciate that there is considerable concern in many walks of life in the Republic about the approach of the Fianna Fáil Government towards United Kingdom and Agentinian involvement in the Falklands.

Unfortunately Mr Desmond did not clarify what he meant by 'many walks of life'. Did he mean Dublin 4? Or Dublin Inner City? Maybe he should consult his Labour colleague, Mr Tom Dalyell MP.

But perhaps the final quote should be left to *Magill* magazine, September 1984:

This woman (Thatcher) caused the death of 368 men, almost all of them young men in their teens and early twenties, for no reason other than that she thought this would win her votes. The luckier ones were blown instantly to smithereens. Others roasted to death in the bowels of the ship or drowned in freezing water.

When she arrives in Dublin for the EEC summit in November will any cabinet minister refuse to meet her on the ground that she uses violence to achieve political ends?

The Tanaiste and Leader of the Labour Party Mr Dick Spring might usefully ponder that question.

4. The Gregory Deal

Tony Gregory is one of a group of young rising Irish politicians who have reacted sharply against the old style Irish politics, so full of verbosity and empty promises. Appalled at the poverty and neglect of Dublin's inner city he and some of his young colleagues campaigned for several years to improve the lot of the people living there. This involved all kinds of semi-political activities, such as meetings, protests, dealings with public bodies like Dublin Corporation, of which he was a member. When, therefore, in the 1982 election he was elected TD he was not a greenhorn or wet behind the ears, but a capable, tough, experienced negotiator and activist. He was elected to look after the interests of the poverty-stricken people of Dublin's inner city and he prepared to tackle that problem with determination and energy. Then by a strange caprice of electoral fortune he found himself cast in the unforeseen role of kingmaker. His vote could decide who would form the next government; Charles Haughey and Fianna Fáil or Garret FitzGerald and Fine Gael.

Gregory did not panic or let his newly-found importance go to his head. His primary duty was not to any political party or ideology but to the people of Dublin's inner city. After these interests were served political ideologies might or might not find a place. Various politicians contacted him and, together with his young advisers, he drew up a plan for inner city improvements. This plan formed the basis for his negotiations with the political leaders. After a number of meetings, modifications, subtractions and additions Charles Haughey accepted the plan and Gregory agreed to vote for him, thus ensuring that Fianna Fáil would form the next government.

Certain sections of the media went almost hysterical. No epithet was bad enough for Haughey. He was a gangster, an Al Capone, an opportunist. His deal with Gregory would cost the Irish taxpayers millions of pounds. He was prepared to gamble this money in pursuit of personal aggrandisement and ambition, etc. etc. It had all been said before except that now it could be related to a price – millions of pounds. (I personally recall similar words of abuse being hurled at De Valera when he concluded the Anglo-Irish Agreement of 1938 and agreed to pay ten million pounds to the British in settlement of outstanding land annuity claims.)

When, however, we look calmly and reasonably at the arrangement we will see the *realpolitik* coming to the surface – the *realpolitik* which the media forgot to emphasise. *Haughey was not the only one to negotiate with Tony Gregory.* But he was the only one who seemed to have a grasp of the realities, and he deeply impressed Gregory and his advisers as a man of ability, acumen, and reliability. Haughey succeeded where the others failed.

Michael O'Leary was then leader of the Labour Party. At his request Gregory and his team held discussions with O'Leary at Wynns Hotel. He would naturally like to have Gregory's vote for the Coalition of which he was a minister. But O'Leary seemed unsure, uncertain and by no means clear on the issues involved.

The noble and righteous profile of Garret FitzGerald projected by the handlers would lead one to believe that he would never stoop to the point of even negotiating on a deal in return for a vote. This would surely be inconsistent with his high sense of uprightness. But curiously enough the image manufactured by the handlers and the *realpolitik* of a situation do not always coincide. *FitzGerald did negotiate and negotiated long and hard.*

At a meeting with Gregory and his advisers at Leinster House Gregory handed FitzGerald the same document as he had previously handed to Haughey. There was a brief discussion and FitzGerald asked for time to consider it. It is important to note here that he did not tell Gregory that he was sorry his principles would not allow him to negotiate a deal for a vote. *The principle of a deal for a vote was accepted.* It was now only a matter of price. FitzGerald's halo had fallen off but the media somehow did not notice it. Some days later, and only a few days before the crucial vote in Dáil Éireann, Garret FitzGerald and Jim Mitchell travelled across the city to Tony Gregory's office in Summerhill. Their meeting lasted over three hours and they spent those hours discussing Gregory's demands. By and large, with few exceptions, they saw no vital reasons why many of these demands should not be met, but FitzGerald was too vague, too woolly, and seemed to lack any clear grasp of the problems of inner Dublin. He seemed to be more at home with the people and problems of Dublin 4. In the end they decided for Haughey. They saw in him the abler politician with a clearer grasp of realities. But FitzGerald was quite willing to make a deal if he could. The harsh fact is that he failed.

Also overlooked by the media was the fact that FitzGerald subsequently made a deal with the Labour Party, in return for their votes, a deal which cost the Irish taxpayer not millions, but billions of pounds – a deal which foisted on the country some of the most stupid policies ever conceived.

Again the vital question raises its head: Why did some of the media consider Haughey dishonourable to make a deal with Tony Gregory for the alleviation of inner city poverty and at the same time saw nothing wrong with Garret FitzGerald trying to make a similar deal, failing and subsequently making a deal costing billions of pounds with the Labour party in return for their votes?

This question remains unanswered.

5. The Case of Seán Doherty

A quite extraordinary aspect of much of the media at the time
was the unusual and indeed inexplicable way they highlighted
trivial matters, if such matters were likely to bring discredit on
Charles Haughey, while at the same time playing down much
more serious matters affecting the very existence of the whole
nation if such were likely to discredit the British or Fine Gael.

Seán Doherty, the Minister for Justice, was one of those
singled out for very unfair and unjust treatment.

Doherty was portrayed as a shifty kind of trickster, who should
never have been given office let alone be made Minister for
Justice. This is a fairly standard line in the methods of vilification.
How many times was it said of Seán Lemass that he was unsuited
for office? When I was researching this book, I checked out that
image of Doherty fairly thoroughly. I interviewed three different
categories of people: (1) those who worked under him, such as
gardaí, and civil servants; (2) his colleagues in the political parties; and (3) a sample of his constituents. Those I interviewed
gave me a very different picture from the projected one. In all
three categories he had his critics and there were many who
disagreed with him, but the vast majority spoke of him as being
an extremely capable minister – indeed some claimed he was
one of the best Ministers for Justice we ever had – a very able
administrator and a strict but fair superior. I tried to find
evidence that he promoted people in the gardaí because they
were political supporters of his, but I was unable to find any.
On the contrary, I found evidence that he refused to promote
people except when such promotion was recommended by their
superiors. I also found ample evidence that he did various
favours for his constituents where he could, but he was honest
enough to admit this and said he would continue to do so as
long as he was in public life. There was a suggestion that he
overdid this to the extent of causing some degree of anxiety
particularly in his constituency. I could find no evidence of this
and his magnificent showing at elections seemed to say that his
constituents had an unusual high degree of confidence and trust

in him.

However, during this research I came across something which looked to me very unusual. There seemed to be a particularly strong venom directed his way during one general election. Often when he addressed a public meeting he was subjected to an unusal amount of heckling and personal abuse. This seemed to occur with unaccountable frequency so that one could not help suspecting it was organised. Again, posters began to appear all over his constituency saying: VOTE NO. 1 TOWEY AND NO. 2 DOHERTY. The reference here was to a gentleman, Andrew Towey, who was alleged to have left Ireland in somewhat of a hurry and whose meat business owed some millions of pounds to small farmers, many of whom were in Doherty's constituency. The implication in these posters was that Doherty was in some way responsible which, of course, was false. Who printed and distributed these posters is unknown. What was also somewhat strange was that I saw no media condemnation of these posters.

Why Doherty should be singled out for such treatment we will discuss later. Suffice it to say here that he was a protègé of Haughey, young, energetic and capable. By throwing dirt at Doherty, one therefore threw dirt at Haughey's judgment. This is one of the oldest ploys.

Apart from the telephone tapping the main ball fired at Doherty was that he tried to fix things for his constituents. The principal one of these charges was that Mr Doherty tried to stop a prosecution against a publican for being open after hours. Mr Doherty has publicly denied this. If one takes into account the accuracy of other media charges against Mr Doherty then one has little difficulty in believing him. Even if there were any truth in the allegation – and those who made it are not rushing forward with proof – and even if Doherty were to stand condemned for it, then this in itself would be a mass condemnation of the majority of Irish TDs and cabinet ministers. Every Irishman and woman knows that the ministers and TDs of every party spend most of their time trying to fix things for their constituents. Indeed some Coalition ministers might well be able to give Seán Doherty a few lessons in this field. I cannot see very much wrong with 'fixing' provided it does not cause injustice. It is really negotiation on behalf of another person who would find it hard to do it himself. It is as old and as legitimate as anything in human history.

Unfortunately the media let us down here again. One would imagine from reading their righteous sentences and listening to their pompous homilies, that Seán Doherty was the only one who ever attempted to halt a prosecution – if he ever did so. If they don't know that this goes on all the time then they should resign their jobs and head for the nearest monastery. I'm told there is no shortage of vacancies.

Perhaps one of the worst pieces of venom directed against Seán Doherty came to be known as the Dowra affair. He was accused of squaring the RUC to have a witness arrested in the Six Counties – a witness who was to give evidence against Mr Doherty's brother-in-law, Garda Nangle, in a court in the Republic. Despite the most exhaustive inquiries by the gardaí nothing has been forthcoming to prove this allegation. Not only that, but the head of the RUC in Northern Ireland, Sir John Hermon had this to say:

> James McGovern was lawfully arrested by the RUC. . . Contrary to reports which have appeared in the news media the Commissioner of the Garda Síochána has stated in writing that he has no complaint against the RUC. . . I know that the Garda Síochána was informed of the arrest of McGovern before the court proceedings in Dowra. . .

If I understand the English language correctly this statement clears Seán Doherty of the alleged complicity in this affair. Furthermore it puts the blame fair and square on the media for publishing a story that could have been misleading, damaging and inaccurate.

But there could be a far more sinister element in the Dowra affair than at first meets the eye. A responsible Northern newspaper published material about Dowra which could only be described as dynamite. The paper suggested that the arrest of McGovern was a ploy to discredit Doherty and was planned and carried out by the RUC Special Branch under the supervision of the British Secret Service (perhaps without informing the Chief Constable). By arresting Mr McGovern on the morning of Garda Nangle's trial, so that he could not travel to court as a witness, it would look as if Doherty arranged it and would consequently discredit him in the eyes of the public. This was allegedly part of the famous OPERATION BROGUE.

There are here a number of elements which should be looked at very, very closely.

Seán Doherty has consistently and vehemently denied that he ever approached the RUC to arrest Mr McGovern. It is also a fact that those who say he did have been quite reluctant to come forward with any proof. Doherty is a very shrewd man and it is unlikely that he would make use of a stupid and highly dangerous ploy to score a point in a trivial matter. In fact his instincts and character would urge him to distance himself as far as possible from a case involving a close relative. In an RTÉ interview Doherty said: 'My brother-in-law – I'm not his keeper – it's as simple as that.' Again as Minister for Justice he was in a position of great influence and most unlikely to want help from the RUC.

That the British Secret Service should try to destroy Doherty seems quite probable. He was one of the principal men responsible for Haughey's election. He was loyal to him. He was in the sensitive Ministry for Justice. *He was engaged in a full scale investigation into the activities of the British Secret Service in his own department* – an investigation which might easily do them immense damage and destroy OPERATION BROGUE. He had begun another investigation into the suspected activities of British agents in semi-state companies like RTÉ. He also began investigating British multi-nationals where many executives were believed to have been former members of MI6. He began to reduce gardaí on border duty and to deploy them in crime-ridden areas in our cities. The British suspected that he would considerably scale down further cross-border collaboration so vital to themselves and the RUC. There was also the added bonus that destroying Doherty helped to destroy Haughey too. Looked at in this light, it would seem more than prudent that they should destroy him – and what more powerful weapon could they use than the old reliable 'vilification'. This vilification was of such proportions that it would require an entire book to deal with it adequately and I hope this book will be written and published in the near future.

What a great pity the media in the South did not take up all this intriguing material, investigate it and let the Irish public know what really happened. If the Northern newspaper had published material damaging to Doherty would the Irish media have treated it with the same veil of silence? Unfortunately many of them were engaged in another world-shaking event – this time in the Kingdom of Kerry!

In September 1982, Mr Doherty's police escort car skidded and turned upside down in a field near Ballybunion. The media went to town on this one! According to their version Seán Doherty was in the car whooping it up with a distinguished Irish singer. The truth is that Doherty was not next to or near the place and the singer was not even in Ireland. Did anyone who wrote, spoke or implied these lies pause for a moment to consider the feelings of Mrs Doherty or the singer. Did any of the media offer an apology to either or say they were sorry? The car was driven by a lone garda who was subsequently brought to court and acquitted. In court his defence counsel felt it necessary to say that the case was 'riddled with doubt, inconsistency and tainted with politics.' This Kerry affair must surely raise the gravest questions as to the reliability of media reporting of Seán Doherty.

Doherty, however, was not going to be let off lightly. When he was Minister for Justice the gardaí arranged to have a security wall built around his house, together with toilets, etc. for a bodyguard. This was presented to the public as if it were a disgraceful waste of public money. But the media forgot to highlight that walls and security buildings were built at the home of Fine Gael Justice Minister, Jim Mitchell, and at the home of the present Fine Gael Justice Minister, Michael Noonan. The building of such walls is a perfectly normal precaution but why should Seán Doherty's wall come in for such criticism?

In December 1982 Dr Michael Woods, former Minister for Health, spoke publicly on the whole Doherty affair. Before any attack was made on Mr Doherty, they were told that a campaign against him was on the way. Dr Woods described the campaign as 'Goebbels-like' and in most restrained language said that some of the media took the bait.

In presenting these matters I am not simply trying to score off Fine Gael or sections of the media. I find it quite sad that I should have to say what I have said. I know many members of the Fine Gael party who are men and women of integrity and ability and I find it difficult to understand why they, and indeed Young Fine Gael, do not protest at a vile and evil tendency to lie, defame, calumniate and destroy the characters of people for temporary political gain, which has taken over in a big way in the party in recent years. They should learn from the past that it does not produce lasting, good results. It has over-shadowed policy – the policy of putting the country on its feet – which so many expected from Dr FitzGerald. All this tendency is doing is helping the British Secret Service destroy Irishmen.

Writing in the *Sunday Press,* the well-known journalist and writer Desmond Fennell, had this to say:

> It is no longer sufficient to defeat your opponents in a general election. When you win and get into government you look for evidence against them in confidential files. Then you publish it, charge them and leave it to the media to prosecute them. Like its prototype in Nuremberg thirty-seven years ago, it is a retreat from civilised standards to primitive vindictiveness. And just as the trial of the defeated German leaders set a grim precedent for future warfare, Garret FitzGerald's Nuremberg trial of the Fianna Fáil leadership augurs ill for the future of democracy in Ireland.

As leader of the party Garret FitzGerald presides over all this and it is quite possible that he is unaware of some of what is going on, but he cannot turn aside and wash his hands of the matter. If he wants to fight Haughey and Fianna Fáil he should do so on policy, performance and political acumen and he should stamp out any tendencies in Fine Gael to hold on to power by spraying dirt at their opponents, which, however unwittingly, is only doing Britain's dirty work. Hatred has never brought any- thing but evil in its train, and surely we Irish can see the terrible results of hatred on our own doorstep. I am sure Garret FitzGerald himself does not want to perpetuate this hatred.

5. GUBU or BUM-STEER Governments

There was what I have always called a Ballsbridge complex
operating against me.
– GENERAL RICHARD MULCAHY

The old proverb which says that 'it never rains but it pours' was well illustrated when, in the case of Charles Haughey, a series of accidental happenings came so close together that Haughey himself referred to them as grotesque, unbelievable, bizarre and unprecedented. Some of his critics seized on the initial letters of these words and referred to Fianna Fáil as the GUBU government. It was a cheap, foxy little ruse which could have further discredited Haughey, and some of the media, ever alert for something saucy and flippant, fell for it.

One would have hoped that their sense of balance, fair play and accurate reporting might have suggested to them that as time passed there might just be another such government, the Coalition GUBU, one which might very easily outstrip, outclass and even overtake Fianna Fáil in translating into practice these overworked adjectives. Fianna Fáil supporters, interestingly enough, believe there is, but they do not call it GUBU. They call it the 'BUM-STEER' government after the Mountjoy misinformation incident.

Since the media overlooked this, perhaps I may suggest a few incidents involving the Fine Gael Coalition which the media might have looked into more deeply and which might eminently qualify them for a place in the GUBU or BUM-STEER club.

The Day of the Poppies

While the participation of the Irish army in the Poppy Day ceremonies of 1983 received wide publicity in the media and once more set Irishmen attacking Irishmen in the letter columns of the newspapers, the significant political undertones, which the media should have jumped on at once, were scarcely mentioned and the public were fed a line that this was a harmless ceremony attended only by a few doddering Colonel Blimps. To the more perceptive journalists however it was, indeed, far from harmless.

The Royal British Legion was founded by Field Marshal Haig and amongst its aims was to commemorate and glorify British military action, not only on the Western Front but on the streets of Dublin in 1916, in the villages and towns of Ireland in 1918-1921 and in the Catholic ghettos of Belfast and Derry in 1969-1984. The men being commemorated were British soldiers, wherever they fought, wherever they died and in whatever cause, however unjust. To be more specific, those being commemorated included the Black-and-Tans, the SAS, the Parachute Regiment of Bloody Sunday infamy, the present regiments of the British army who have caused over 2,000 deaths in the Six Counties. As a sop to the Irish those who died in the service of the UN would be commemorated but *not* those who fought the British for the freedom of Ireland.

It is important, therefore, to look at those who were *not* commemorated at this ceremony. They include *all* Irish soldiers who fought for their country against the British, men like Michael Collins, Cathal Brugha, Roger Casement, Dan Breen, Eamon de Valera, W. T. Cosgrave and indeed Desmond FitzGerald, father of Garret, who was actually sentenced to six months imprisonment for trying to prevent young Irishmen from joining the same British army now being commemorated. The soldiers who shot Pearse and Connolly were commemorated but not Pearse and Connolly. The soldiers with blackened faces who murdered Lord Mayor Tomás MacCurtain were commemorated but not Tomás MacCurtain. Neither was Kevin Barry commemorated but the men who tortured and hung him were. No Irish soldier who fought or died for his country fighting the British was commemorated but the British soldiers who hunted them down and shot them like rabbits were all commemorated. The British soldiers who stopped at nothing to prevent an Irish army being founded were commemorated but those Irish soldiers who died trying to found our Irish army were not.

Almost since the inception of the state the British have tried to involve the Irish army in these ceremonies but without success. Even as far back as 1925 one of the founding fathers of Fine Gael, Kevin O'Higgins, refused to have any part in them with the curt remark: 'This state has other origins'. Leaders of Fine Gael governments or Coalitions such as W. T. Cosgrave, John A. Costello and Liam Cosgrave also refused, as did various presidents of the state. But the British kept up the pressure and finally in 1983 their persistence paid off when Garret FitzGerald and his Defence Minister, Patrick Cooney, agreed to the Irish army participating in these grotesque ceremonies to honour the soldiers who tried to destroy it.

FitzGerald actively approved of the attendance of the Irish army at this commemoration and when some of Ireland's most distinguished ex-officers such as General M. J. Costello and General Sean McKeown, protested, Mr Cooney, the Fine Gael Defence Minister, dismissed them as 'bigots'.

Indeed when Charles Haughey and Fianna Fáil participated in a commemoration ceremony for Wolfe Tone, whom FitzGerald says is one of his heroes, Mr Cooney, in criticising this ceremony, was reported in a newspaper to have commented: 'We have the now familiar bugler blowing his lugubrious but highly emotive music.' It seems strange that he did not see anything reprehensible in a bugler sounding the last post for British soldiers at Poppy Day ceremonies which he himself attended. Perhaps here the media should have asked the question as to whether Garret FitzGerald and his government consider it reprehensible for a bugler to sound the last post for Wolfe Tone but praiseworthy to sound the last post for the Black-and-Tans?

In any civilised community people and governments should honour the dead of those who opposed them. This idea was put forward by a group of distinguished Irishmen from all walks of life who suggested to Dr FitzGerald that there should be a special commemoration that would honour all Irish soldiers as well as all British soldiers. FitzGerald did not accept the proposal. One would have hoped that the media would have pursued this and would have delved into why Irish soldiers should honour dead British soldiers while the British refused to honour dead Irish soldiers. There were so many interesting and newsworthy questions they could have asked such as: Can one imagine the French army attending a ceremony for the Gestapo only, or the German army attending a ceremony for the Russians only? Why did the British army refuse to attend Easter Week commemorations, or why did the British Minister for Defence, with high-ranking British officers, not attend the annual Easter Week Mass in London? Again why did FitzGerald yield to the British? Did Fine Gael participate as an act of apology for 1916, the War of Independence and our neutrality in 1939-1945? To what extent was Kevin Boland's assertion that Fine Gael was testing public opinion as to how strong the reaction is for or against moving back towards the British Commonwealth and into NATO true? How much support throughout the country was there for Dr C. S. Andrews' assertion that if we had a Taoiseach less determined to please the British then the Minister for Defence would be sacked? Could there be a more grotesque situation than that of an army founded by Michael Collins commemorating the men who tried to kill Collins, and not even a prayer for Collins himself? Could this happen in any self-respecting country in the world? Or have we truly lost our nationhood and become a real banana republic? Surely the media should have asked some of these questions and dealt with them in depth.

It may well be that by the time these lines reach the public some change might have taken place. One of Ireland's most distinguished military leaders and industrialists, General M. J. Costello, has come out of retirement to lead a campaign against Irish army involvement in Poppy Day. Hitherto unknown facts that during the Second World War the British Legion were engaged in intelligence activities as well as in encouraging young soldiers to desert the Irish army have now come to light. According to a television report, an appeal has been made to Dr FitzGerald to stop genuflecting before the British and it may well be that the Taoiseach will recall those Irishmen, including his own father, who fought the British and who were not commemorated – men whose sacrifices made it possible for Dr FitzGerald himself to become Taoiseach. If this is so then General Costello's noble suggestion of a national commemoration day for all soldiers might well become a reality.

British Spies in Ireland

When one tries to write about the activities of British spies in Ireland one enters a dark, murky world which literally stinks. The stories one hears are equally hard either to confirm or reject, yet one instinctively knows most of them have a solid foundation. To get anywhere one has to depend on a mixture of circumstantial evidence, contacts not exactly high-up in the establishment, the revelations of ex-spies and the occasional blunder. By a patient piecing together of information from all these sources one may get some rags of truth.

Britain never fully accepted that Ireland is an independent nation and she sees us as a recalcitrant corner of the mainland that might one day have to be invaded and chastised. Hence the necessity for spies to keep her informed on the likely opposition to or support for such an eventuality. But spying in Ireland became far more intensified with the advent of the Troubles in the Six Counties and with the establishment of a Russian embassy in Dublin.

It is now estimated that approximately fifty or sixty British spies work full time in the Republic of Ireland. How many part-time spies is unknown but the figure may well run into hundreds. Also unknown is how many British spies come down from the North at irregular intervals posing as businessmen and set up phoney businesses as cover. The ease with which these people can operate here is most surprising. I know for a certainty, for example, that two of Mr Haughey's staff were approached by the British Secret Service to work for them. They refused. Were others in Fianna Fáil asked?

A young Irishman, partly blackmailed by the British to work for them, told his story to the *Irish Press* who published it in July 1982. This man gave details of whom he was supposed to watch and report on and he also gave details of some of the activities of British spies, particularly in the Parnell Square area of Dublin. When he decided to pack up and leave the country he confessed his activities to Irish army intelligence and the gardaí. He was subsequently interviewed by a garda inspector who gave him little satisfaction and told him to go home and keep his mouth shut. Surely the media might have tried to find out if this inspector was acting on government orders, or not.

The case of Tony and Margaret Hayde is now well known. They were lured to Spain on a free holiday and there approached by British agents who offered them £10,000 to act as informers in Ireland. Scores of cases have come to light over the past fifteen years of the operation of British spies in the Republic.

Again the media might well have investigated the suspicions that on the roof of the British embassy in Dublin there is a monitor which can tap into telephone calls between government ministers and phone calls between the Department of External Affairs and Irish embassies abroad. If this is so, why is it being permitted to remain there? Because it is the British embassy?

It is, of course, true to say that this kind of thing goes on all the time in most European countries, but what is peculiar about Ireland is the allegation that the Coalition government know of all this and has taken no effective steps to stop it. If this is true, surely it is unprecedented in the history of the state. To investigate matters like this and tell the whole truth is surely the function of a free and unbiased media.

A number of disturbing articles appeared in Northern Irish newspapers to the effect that there were vast sums of money available to bribe people to get rid of Charles Haughey and take over Fianna Fáil. They reported that this money, which ran well into six figures, was supplied by the British Secret Service to an Irish business firm to distribute, so that the source could not be detected. They also stated that a number of bogus business companies were set up in Ireland for a similar purpose. Now these reports may be true or false, but again one would expect the media in the South to have picked them up and investigated them.

Do the Coalition turn a blind eye to all this? Or are they simply incompetent? They expelled three Russian diplomats for alleged activities *outside* the boundaries of the Republic. Did they tell the truth about why they expelled them? How could they be spying on nuclear installations in the North when we have the word of the British that there are no such nuclear installations there? Were they expelled because they made a deal with the IRA to give them the names and addresses of the re-settled supergrasses in return for certain information about nuclear activity in the North? Have the CIA been allowed to purchase buildings near the Russian embassy. If so, why are they not expelled? Why do the Coalition not take more effective steps to stop British spies operating within the boundaries of the Republic?

If Charles Haughey and Seán Doherty expelled three *British* diplomats for spying and at the same time gave the KGB comparatively free rein in the country, what would the media do?

Here I think it is important to say that one should never get too obsessed with tales of secret agents and spies. On the other hand, one should not turn a blind eye to very obvious pointers. When agents are being trained they are instructed to pour scorn on people who are on their trail by saying such people are paranoid, etc. The Russians worked that one with great success in Britain where, at one time, even to suggest that there were Russian spies about was considered a form of madness. Nevertheless these questions have a great relevance for the Irish people and one would hope that the media, who have vast resources at their disposal, have a duty not to leave them in the dark.

The Reagan Circus

From time to time foreign statesmen visit our country on what has now come to be known as state visits. There is usually a lot of ballyhoo, laudatory speeches, cultural visits and state dinners on these occasions. It would, however, be a simpleton who would believe that these political visitors come here because they love us, or because they want to kiss the Blarney Stone. The harsh *realpolitik* is that they all want something.

Now there is nothing particularly wrong with that provided they are prepared to pay the price and give something in return. Usually both countries have, through their officials, discussed in advance what concessions each wants from the other so that when the visit takes place there is broad general agreement and the visit becomes an occasion for polishing off details, shaking hands and making public pronouncements. Of course, if there is no agreement in advance, then there is no visit.

When President Reagan came to Ireland in June 1984, he wanted something and he wanted it very badly. He wanted to be re-elected president of the United States and to help him in that task he wanted the votes of forty million people of Irish descent in that country. They would see the television coverage on their screens and through this coverage he would show them that he was one of themselves from the ould sod, that he travelled all the way to Ireland, and especially to Ballyporeen to find his roots and to worship at the shrine of his forefathers, like so many of those of Irish descent had done before him. He was cunning enough to make a special broadcast to the American people from dear old Erin's Isle and, in true crude, stage-Irish style, he started off with 'the top of the morning to you' and continued:

> Those of you like me, who can claim the good fortune of Irish roots may appreciate the tug I felt yesterday when we saw the Emerald Isle from Airforce I. . .

This, of course, was a lot of codswallop, drivel and nonsense. The only tug he felt was the tug of those millions of Irish votes he hoped to capture in the election. He had been three times in Ireland before and he never bothered his head to visit Ballyporeen or search for his Irish roots, which are, to put it mildly, historically very tenuous. But on this occasion he wanted those votes so badly that every exploitation of the shillelagh, shamrock, round tower and wolfhound was permissable. At the worst the whole visit was an insult to the intelligence of the Irish people; at the best it threw into focus the blundering, political ineptitude of the Irish government who played along all the way with this Barnum-like circus.

One would have hoped that Garret FitzGerald, as leader of the Irish people, would have insisted on an effective quid-pro-quo exercise; that he would have said to Reagan, 'Unless you publicly call in the strongest possible words for an immediate political initiative leading to a withdrawal of British troops from Northern Ireland the visit is off and you can stay at home.'

This is the kind of language Reagan would understand. It is the kind of language any European statesman would have used in similar circumstances. It is the kind of language De Valera or Lemass would have used.

Unfortunately this did not happen. Like our grovelling before the British, we grovelled before Reagan and he got everything he wanted, on an official level, without giving one iota in return.

What was even worse, he made use of his visit here to do what Margaret Thatcher wished him to do, namely, to publicly condemn Northern Republicans, while remaining silent on the British 'shoot-to-kill' policy, the plastic bullets, the Russian-style courts, the paid informers and the Castlereagh-type torture in our own El Salvador not many miles from where he was speaking. No wonder Thatcher was delighted with his voicing her policy on Irish soil. No wonder she praised him publicly for standing by her, and when he left Ireland with everything he wanted, the Irish government, to pay for this visit, dipped into the taxpayers purse for close on two million pounds at a time when the statistics showed a million of our population on the bread-line. Even in those circumstances it might be worth it if we got something in return. And as if to add insult to injury our government allowed American security forces, who accompanied Reagan, to take over from our gardaí, to bully, browbeat and humiliate them at every opportunity. They established a kind of KGB type of ascendancy in the village of Ballyporeen, illegally searched houses, and acted as if they owned the place, without a whisper of protest from the Coalition. This led one cynical commentator to remark:

> This is a grave departure in the independence of our security forces. Usually they only take orders from British agents.

All this, of course, raised the question of what Charlie Haughey would have done were he Taoiseach. Well in advance of Reagan's visit he seems to have made it quite clear that he would not let Reagan get away with very much. A short time previously the American Secretary of State, George Shultz, speaking at the Stockholm disarmament conference said:

> The United States does not recognise the legitimacy of the artificially imposed division of Europe. . . the attempt to impose division on Europe is inevitably a source of instability and tension. . . Germany was one of Europe's great nations heartlessly divided.

Taking up this speech by one of Reagan's right-hand men, Haughey had this to say:

Would it not be one of those noble and generous acts, which have happened from time to time in American history and the final tribute to the enormous contribution the ancestors of forty million Irish-Americans have made in the building of America and to the valuable part they have played and still play in the political life of that democracy, if the President, in addressing both houses of the Irish parliament in June, were to declare that the United States does not recognise 'the legitimacy of the artificially imposed division' of Ireland either and that henceforth the United States will include the re-establishment of the historic unity of Ireland as a major objective of her foreign policy.

These words would seem to spell out loud and clear that there would be no bonus for Reagan if he were not prepared to commit himself to the condemnation of the artificial division of our country. He must have thanked his stars that FitzGerald, not Haughey, was Taoiseach! He had got everything he wanted and gave nothing in return.

The last act in this bizarre circus seemed to highlight Fine Gael's fear and terror of Mr Haughey. Every chance they got during the visit they tried to humiliate and embarrass him – from the seating arrangements in Galway, to the attempt not to introduce him to Reagan in the Dáil, to the final insult at Dublin airport where, despite an official invitation from Aer Rianta, they tried to prevent him seeing Reagan off. How strangely that shabby conduct contrasts with the courtesy extended by Seán Lemass to the leaders of Fine Gael and Labour right through the visit of President Kennedy. This is just one more example of a petty nastiness which has crept into Fine Gael, a kind of offensive repulsiveness which is strangely inconsistent with the high moral rectitude projected by the handlers.

As the curtain fell on this undignified circus the greatest turn of all was kept to the end – a dinner paid for by the Irish taxpayer, which looked more like a Fine Gael reunion party than a national occasion to honour a state guest. But the hard, tough common sense of the Irish prevailed. The list of those who did not attend was much more impressive than those who did and included the names of some of the most prominent and distinguished people in the public life of the nation – a bizarre comment on GUBU or BUM-STEER government.

Here again the media should have alerted the public to what was afoot. It was not just enough to report the ballyhoo of the visit. The deeper implication of it should have been brought to the attention of the public; how the Irish people were exploited at their own expense in order to benefit an unco-operative foreign political leader and the negligence or stupidity of the government in allowing this to happen.

The FitzGerald Dimension

While the media have examined the career of Charlie Haughey inside out and upside down, they have failed to engage in another examination which might very well highlight matters affecting our whole future as a free and independent nation. For want of a better description, I have called that element *The FitzGerald Dimension*. It concerns Dr FitzGerald's public image as projected by the handlers and his actions and the actions of his party. The two do not always coincide. Indeed at times the divergence reaches unbelievable proportions.

Every aspect of Charles Haughey's life has come under the searchlight of the media and the pattern I mentioned before seems to emerge. Material embarrassing to Haughey or to Republicanism seems to be highlighted, while serious matters likely to embarrass the British or Fine Gael or Garret FitzGerald tend to be toned down or quietly ignored.

The media searchlight has as yet not been turned on Garret FitzGerald. Where he has committed major political blunders the media, as a whole, have treated him gently and even at times gone so far as to make excuses for him. No such generous spirit has been shown to Haughey.

One of the reasons put forward for this is that FitzGerald is pleasant and friendly with the media and Haughey is not. It would be a great pity if this were true because it implies that the political leadership of our country might well depend on how well one studied and absorbed Dale Carnegie's *How to Win Friends and Influence People*. Surely the Irish public should not have to depend for their information on the pleasantness shown to the media by political leaders? Surely they have a right to expect the whole truth. In the affairs of a nation where the lives of millions of ordinary people are concerned these lives should not depend on the smiles of politicians. De Valera, de Gaulle and Lincoln were not exactly the darlings of the media. Indeed a correspondent in the *Guardian* newspaper, with typical arrogance, said: 'It was a shock to find Mr Haughey behaving in the manner of Mr De Valera in World War II.' The implication here is that since De Valera's day we have moved much closer to the British point of view, and should behave ourselves accordingly.

Some cynics say that journalists have an inferiority complex when confronted by an academic or a professor like FitzGerald – a complex they do not have when faced with a non-professor like Haughey. If there is any truth in this they can easily remind themselves that, with the possible exception of Salazar, no professor or academic ever led his nation into anything but chaos.

Is Garret FitzGerald leading Ireland into chaos? That is a question which it is high time the media dealt with, thoroughly and in depth, and in this section I suggest certain lines of inquiry that they might usefully pursue.

One of the charges most often levelled against FitzGerald is that he is a kind of West Briton who accepts the British as a superior race and who can usually be counted upon, in so far as it is politically possible, to see things the British way, especially in relation to the Six Counties.

One of those who levelled this charge against him was Charles Haughey:

> In return for the support he has given British policy, British spokesmen, TV, radio and newspapers are now making clear their support for him.

Again Mr Haughey came back to the attack after Peter Barry made a particularly nationalistic speech:

> I wish to put the question clearly to Dr FitzGerald: Is it in fact correct that he apologised or made excuses to Mrs Thatcher for a speech made in Limerick by the Minister for Foreign Affairs, Mr Peter Barry? Is it correct that he told the British Prime Minister to disregard Mr Barry's statement that he wanted to see an eventual fading out of the British involvement in Irish affairs and that she was not to take seriously his statement that he regarded 'the long-

term British presence in Ireland as an obstacle to the reconciliation of the two traditions'?

Mr Haughey further stated that Fine Gael's collaboration amounted to the *most serious threat to the Republic's political independence since the Second World War.*

Gerry Collins, Fianna Fáil Minister for Foreign Affairs was another who attacked Dr FitzGerald on this score. Mr Collins said that the British establishment wanted Dr FitzGerald to win the election because they expected Fine Gael support for British policy in the North. He also said that there was secret collusion between Dr FitzGerald and the British concerning the North and that the Fine Gael proposals for an all-Ireland police force could lead to the RUC turning up on the doorsteps in Donegal and Kerry.

Mr Gene FitzGerald, Fianna Fáil's Minister for Finance, also publicly criticised Dr FitzGerald:

> By consistently pandering to the British view of Anglo-Irish rela-
> tions and acting in accordance with British interests Dr FitzGerald
> is in grave danger of joining a select London club of 'great and
> good Irishmen' always ready to receive applause from the other
> side of the water for representing the Irish government and people
> and their aspirations to maximum disadvantage.

But perhaps even more telling is a newspaper report of September 1982 that a former Senator, a distinguished and prominent member of the Fine Gael party, resigned from the party and denounced its present leadership as 'pro-British'. If this report is correct then it may well reflect the suspicion of many other prominent members of the Fine Gael party.

Other instances have been put forward as examples, such as the spending of two hundred and fifty million pounds a year to protect British interests here, his stand with Britain on the Malvinas issue, his ready acquiescence to British demands for extradition.

It has also been alleged that Fine Gael are ultimately a Commonwealth party committed to our returning to the empire with a Governor General, Oath of Allegiance and all the usual trappings. As a young university student I myself heard W. T. Cosgrave state in Eyre Square, Galway, when he was recommending the rejection of the Constitution that: 'It is the aim of our party that Ireland should be a good member of the British Common-wealth.' Again, according to an article in the *Sunday Times* in December 1983, Fine Gael circulated a document to members of the Forum which advised that membership of the Common-wealth should be discussed. It apparently came to a sudden end when Haughey exclaimed 'No way'.

Now all these matters, the allegations that he is a West Briton and that he wants to bring us back into the Commonwealth should be thoroughly investigated by the media. If they are true then the Irish public have a right to know who is leading them. If they are untrue then it is only fair to FitzGerald himself and to the party that this should be so stated.

I have studied carefully the actions, speeches and writings of Michael Collins and I am unable to find any one issue where he would agree with the present leadership of Fine Gael. A media investigation into Fine Gael and Michael Collins would be very enlightening for the Irish public.

Nowhere does Garret FitzGerald's alleged leaning towards the British come across so clearly as in his basic attitude towards the North. The British have put out a superb propaganda line which they have successfully propagated all over the world, namely, that the problem in Northern Ireland is the reconcilia-tion of two traditions and that is what Britain is trying to do. FitzGerald's critics say that he has fully and totally swallowed that line – a line that is as false as it is nonsensical.

The problem in Northern Ireland is, not as FitzGerald has said, complicated and complex but very simple and straightfor-ward. The British need Northern Ireland for military and strategic reasons and it does not matter what the Unionists think, what the Nationalists think, what the people of the Republic think, Britain will hold on to Northern Ireland as long as it is militarily necessary. That strategic necessity, his critics say, seems to have eluded FitzGerald completely. He seems unable to grasp the fundamental truth that it is the British, and not the IRA nor Fianna Fáil, nor the Unionists, who are the first cause of most of our problems, and who are the real subversives. One would hope that, political problems aside, their recent actions on the Milk Levy and Kinsale Gas would convince him that they will always crush anything likely to be of major economic benefit to us. But this does not seem to register with FitzGerald. He seems unaware of the widespread British campaign abroad to undermine confidence in the Irish economy. The prestigious American magazine *Business Week* said in November 1982:

> Irish officials are convinced that the Thatcher government is trying to undermine Haughey – and international bankers' confidence in Ireland's credit – by depicting Ireland as an insolvent borrower. 'There is an outrageous attempt to put Ireland in the same class as Poland and Mexico,' says Padraic A. White, managing director of Ireland's Industrial Development Authority.

This is but one quotation of several from prestigious journals and newspapers which more than prove that this British campaign to break international confidence in Ireland is in full swing. But FitzGerald seems oblivious to it all.

We are to be kept as serfs. The British have simply used the Unionists over the past sixty years to rule that statelet for them, irrespective of what brutality had to be used, and she is now supporting them because they are the best bet to enable her to hold on to the statelet. She is holding on to it by force, she intends to hold on to it by force and the harsh *realpolitik* of the situation is that we are helping her to do this with our army, with our police force and with our courts. No amount of whitewashing or high-sounding speech-making can change that fact. It is the old story: 'Set the Paddies at each other's throats and we'll bury the pieces.' I think it was the late Lord Birkenhead who said: 'War by the Irish on the Irish gives me particular satisfaction.' If FitzGerald's critics are right then he is collaborating, however unwittingly, in that policy and this is something the media might examine in depth.

'I believe passionately in a united Ireland, and I believe in the principles enunciated by Tone and Davis,' Dr FitzGerald said in 1982. Here was a glorious opportunity for the media to look up the principles of Tone and Davis and relate them to FitzGerald's actions regarding the Irish language and the connection with England. His passionate belief in a united Ireland should be related to an item in the *Irish Times* in May 1984 where it was suggested that FitzGerald's preference, in a federated Ireland, would be for the British monarch to remain as head of the Northern State. So in a united, federated Ireland we would have two heads of state – the British monarch in the North whether or not the Nationalists wanted it – and the president in the South. What kind of a muddled and confused united Ireland that would make should have intrigued the media.

In Washington British officials expressed sheer delight at FitzGerald's address to Congress. They felt that in political matters they could always rely on him to see things the British way. His approach to Northern Ireland delights them particularly. He believes that you cannot force 800,000 Unionists into a united Ireland but apparently it is quite all right to force 650,000 Nationalists into a sectarian British state against their will. Again Dr FitzGerald tells us: 'Our laws, constitution and our practices are not acceptable to the Protestants of Northern Ireland.' The media might well have asked him: So what? Are the laws and constitution of Northern Ireland acceptable to 650,000 Nationalists? Are the laws and constitution of West Germany acceptable to the Russians and communists of East Germany? Must West Germany change her laws to satisfy the communists before the country can be united? Must Spain change her laws to satisfy the British in Gibraltar?

Perhaps the media should have asked him a question about the laws and constitution under which these 650,000 Catholics are forced to live – discrimination, torture, supergrasses, Diplock courts. Should we change our laws to fall in line with the British? Britain is the most sectarian country in Western Europe. The Church of England is established by law. The king or queen must, by law, be a Protestant. Prince Charles could not marry a Catholic. Would Dr FitzGerald like us to fall in line with those laws?

He should be asked if he realises that for sixty years the Unionists have had ninety per cent of the goodies – jobs, housing, money – and they intend to hold on to them. It is unlikely that it is for the marketing of contraceptives, the right to divorce, the liberalising of a constitution they are fighting, but for their powers, their highly-paid jobs, their privileges which they refuse to share with the rest of the population.

One area where Dr FitzGerald's righteous words sound puzzling is when he said: 'My job is to persuade the Irish people to adopt the principles of Tone and Davis.'

The media should really have asked how he has gone about putting the principles of Tone and Davis into effect. By extraditing young Irishmen and handing them over to a police force so evil and corrupt that it is the only police force in Western Europe that shares with the Gestapo the odium of having been condemned by an International Court for cruelty and torture – a police force that has tortured thousands of Irishmen and women and forced them through the most excruciating torments to sign lying and false confessions? Would Tone and Davis have approved of the Diplock courts, which rely on the evidence of paid informers, which have sentenced innocent men and women to savage terms of imprisonment – worse indeed than the Moscow trials of the thirties – courts which the most responsible Legal Associations have roundly condemned? What would be the attitude of Tone and Davis to a government that tolerated a situation where trained British killers could cross the border seemingly as often as they wished, abduct young Irishmen and in some cases murder them? How would Tone and Davis react to the contempt shown to the Irish language at every level of Irish life?

These are but a few of the questions the media might have asked and they could have done a great service for the Irish public by extracting from the writings of Tone and Davis those principles which could be seen to justify the many unbelievable actions of Dr FitzGerald's Coalition.

Perhaps too they might have cast a glance at another allegation often made against Garret FitzGerald, namely, that he and his government are paranoid in their attitude to Republicanism. Perhaps the most outstanding example of this is FitzGerald's refusal to meet and discuss common affairs with members of Sinn Féin. The reason given for this is that members of Sinn Féin have not renounced violence.

In September 1983 he received Robert Mugabe with full honours – as indeed it should be. Mugabe led one of the bloodiest struggles ever with the armalite and the ballot box. Was he asked did he renounce violence before he was received in audience?

In an interview with the *Cork Examiner* in September 1981 Garret FitzGerald said he would be glad to meet Ian Paisley and welcome him in Dublin, but he would *not* meet Owen

Carron, the elected MP for South Tyrone. Did he ask Paisley if he renounced violence? Could he give one single quote from Paisley's speeches to show he renounced violence? Did he ever hear of Paisley's Third Force, or see photographs of them? Perhaps he should note a comment made recently by former Fine Gael finance minister, Ritchie Ryan MEP: 'A verbal terrorist like Paisley is as guilty of deaths in Northern Ireland as any man who pulls a trigger.' Does he approve of the meetings which took place between members of a Fine Gael cabinet and the UDA? Were they asked if they renounced violence? Some UDA prisoners in Irish gaols were visited privately by members of the Fine Gael party. One can only praise them for this thoughtful and charitable act. I may be misinformed, but I have no knowledge of any IRA prisoners being privately visited in the same way by members of Fine Gael. Can one say that Dr FitzGerald approves of this kind of distinction, if it exists? He too, when in England, visited a British soldier in hospital, but apparently did not consider visiting Irish prisoners in English jails. Is it so with Fine Gael that the followers of Pádraig Pearse and Michael Collins are to get the boot, while the followers of Carson and Brookeborough are to get the red carpet.

When Henry Kissinger came to Dublin Garret FitzGerald received him with full red carpet honours. Did he ask Kissinger about 15,000 deaths he was responsible for in Cambodia? Did he ask him to renounce violence before he was received? In the light of the new information on the *Belgrano* will he now refuse to meet Thatcher? These are some of the questions the media might usefully have asked. Brendan Behan once said that if you plant small bombs and kill a few people you are a terrorist. If you drop big bombs and massacre thousands you are a statesman. Which was Kissinger? Reagan? Thatcher?

In examining his supposed leanings towards the British, the media might take a look at what seems to be Garret FitzGerald's extraordinary capacity for accepting insults from the British in the practical domain. True, they praise him in their media, but in the practical domain of *realpolitik* they seem to boot him around as they wish. It is as if their support for him is the same as the support the rope gives the hanging man; when it suits them they will cut it and let the body drop into the quicklime.

One insult after another has been proffered. Margaret

Thatcher, the Duke of Edinburgh, Princess Margaret, Prince Charles visited discredited units of the British army in the North. Each time our government sent a protest. Each time it was ignored. The typewriters of the Department of Foreign Affairs must by now be worn out typing protests, and if Britain ultimately invades Ireland we can be sure of another 'low-key protest.' Surely a leader of calibre should not have to be told what to do after the first protest had been ignored? Exasperated at what seemed to be FitzGerald's inability to see through the British, Haughey arraigned him across the floor of the Dáil:

> Will you never learn? Will you never understand that no matter what soft words or protestations are used the age-old reality prevails? Britain relentlessly and remorselessly pursues British self-interest no matter whom it hurts or effects.

Finally the media might ask if, after two years of government, the image of Garret FitzGerald presented to the public – the image of a young, modern liberal who would lead us to the promised land – still holds good; or if the façade has crumbled to reveal an unimaginative, blundering politician in the old blueshirt tradition of confused, insensitive and coercive government.

I do not wish to give the impression that I am trying to denigrate Garret FitzGerald. That is the farthest thing from my mind, but as leader of the nation he should be open to questioning. I am not discussing his worth. He is a man of above average intellect and is possessed of great energy for work, but in the same way as Charles Haughey's suitability for the position of Taoiseach was put into the arena so should his. One would hope, however, that unlike in Haughey's case, the media would do so in a balanced and fair way. Two wrongs do not make a right.

I have only touched on a few instances which would qualify the Coalition government for membership of the GUBU or BUM-STEER Club. There are scores of others: the Ballinamore fiasco where a few untrained paramilitaries ran rings round hoards of our soldiers and police and where nobody knows, as yet, who fired the fatal shots; the Amendment farce; the shame of extradition; cross-border incursions; the Mountjoy misinformation; the deals with the Labour party, because of which we cannot get any industrialist to invest in this country. The list is endless and must surely, without doubt, go a long way towards qualifying them for perpetual membership of either of the two clubs!

6. The Vital Why

Liberty is the right to tell people what they do not want to hear.
– GEORGE ORWELL

*Give the investigators a hors d'oeuvre and with a little luck
they won't come back for the main course.*
– RICHARD NIXON

For those who govern the first thing required is indifference to newspapers.
– LOUIS TREAS

There can, I am sure, be little doubt now in anyone's mind that large sections of the media allowed themselves to be used in a campaign to denigrate Charles Haughey in such a way that it could have the result of driving him from public life. The evidence is, of course, mostly circumstantial but as Thoreau once said: 'If you buy a gallon of milk and you find a small fish swimming around, you have reason to suspect all is not well.'

We had an old saying in the army that the target is always the best judge of the accuracy of the aim. Mr Haughey was the target and his comment was:

> It is a consistent campaign of news management, of vilification against me personally, and the Fianna Fáil party, a consistent campaign of accusation and falsehood.

As well as that there were responsible people within the media itself who believed that the media were unfair to Haughey. Miss Geraldine Kennedy admitted that there was 'a lot of personal sniping against Charles Haughey which was unfair and could just as equally have been done on Garret FitzGerald and it wasn't.'

A columnist in *The Sunday Press* suggested that a subversive element was operating in RTÉ and the media to undermine the image of Charles Haughey and divide Fianna Fáil. His view was that the benefits would not only go to Fine Gael and Labour but to 'subversives and semi-subversive bodies'.

The political correspondent of the *Cork Examiner* agreed with those who said that:

> there was a virulent media campaign against the Opposition. . .
> and there was a heavy bias shown against Fianna Fáil and particu-
> larly Mr Haughey by an influential section of the Dublin media.

This correspondent referred to the fact that the 'anti-Haughey' mood surfaced most sharply at press conferences. An almost truculent attitude in their questioning of the Fianna Fáil leader was displayed by a couple of journalists. He suggested that this attitude was in marked contrast to the kid-glove handling of Garret FitzGerald.

Seán Duignan, political correspondent of RTÉ said:

> . . . there is no clear evidence that Charles Haughey as a person
> should not lead the Irish people. Even from the dissidents within
> Fianna Fáil there is no specific reason ever given as to why Charlie
> is not a fit person to lead the party or the country – all there are
> are the dark hints that he is unsuitable. I feel the media reflected
> these unstated reservation about Haughey and because they are
> unstated and therefore unsubstantiated they were unfair. . . The
> media should be guided by a remark of a former journalist, 'one's
> primary asset apart from a serene spirit, is a steady resistance to
> moral indignation.'

Now of course we have to ask the sixty-four thousand dollar question, which is at the very core of this book, namely, *Why did such a large section of the media engage in the campaign against Charles Haughey?*

The fact that the British wanted him out at all costs may give us a clue which leads to the question: *Are there paid British spies working in the various branches of the Irish media?* It would be a brave man who would try to answer that question with certainty, but there are a few pointers.

On 22 December 1975 the prestigious *Washington Post* stated that the British Secret Service had some paid agents working as journalists on most British newspapers. A Fleet Street editor revealed that the Secret Service had more than half the staff of one particular newspaper on their payroll. If this is the case in Britain surely one cannot rule out the possibility of some similar involvement in the Irish media – perhaps not to the same extent. Kenneth Lindsay in his book *The British Intelligence Service in Action* says:

> DI6 is responsible for intelligence and covert operations in the Irish Republic and has numerous agents and informants, including many at high level in the civil service, police and armed service. . . *The news media in particular has been infiltrated at all levels. . . by either British or American intelligence* (italics mine).

Lindsay goes on to quote the case of a special agent whom he says is 'a prime mover in what will ultimately be seen as the most ambitious and effective covert operation to *disestablish the Fianna Fáil party and the present Fianna Fáil government'* (italics mine). His book was published in 1980 and it naturally tempts the question: Have we seen it happen?

Patrick FitzGerald, one of the authors of *British Intelligence and Covert Action,* in an interview with Kevin Toolis in the *Sunday Press* in May 1983, said that MI6 has successfully penetrated the Irish media and civil service and runs an extensive spy network in Ireland. They have been fairly successful in influencing government policy, he said, and he further added that the Irish media, according to a reliable British security source, was 'very well penetrated'. He also stated that they paid special attention to 'black propaganda' consisting of lies, smears and false allegations to discredit their opponents. In another interview with David Orr in the *Sunday Independent,* Patrick FitzGerald is quoted as saying:

> In all there are about twenty intelligence officers from MI6 and possibly up to two hundred agents operating in the Republic. Practically every top-level of Irish society has been infiltrated. MI6 hold key positions in all Irish political parties, the gardaí, the army, the civil service and the media. I know at least one producer in RTÉ working directly for British Intelligence.

I do not have sufficient information myself to confirm all that has been said so I can only offer an opinion. If we take into account Britain's track record in other countries, it would be unwise to rule out the possibility that there are some British agents working in important positions in the media and that these agents exercise a disproportionate influence on what is published – the kind of influence that would enable them to carry out a subtle campaign of vilification without leaving any tell-tale tracks behind them.

It would, I suggest, be very foolish for those who own, or are in charge of, media outlets, to ignore that possibility. It has happened in most other countries where Britain had interests so why should Ireland be the exception?

As distinct from direct membership of the British Secret Service, *to what extent was the wool pulled over the eyes of journalists by other means?*

There are over one thousand journalists working in the country and the vast majority of these go about their daily work with efficiency and honesty. It is possible, however, that a number of these had the wool pulled over their eyes within the framework of a superb British flattery-propaganda exercise as part of OPERATION BROGUE. The skill and subtlety of this operation can be judged by the fact that many of the journalists who attacked Charlie Haughey sincerely and honestly believed they were doing the country a service, whereas in reality they may well have been only promoting the British line, without meaning to. Many sections of the media may well have been hoodwinked by an organisation which has hundreds of years of experience of this kind of work behind it and which operates with sinister efficiency in all countries of the world. Again one has to be careful not to get paranoid about this matter and see spies under every bed. Wherever they are they are not under the bed, but keeping a sharp weather-eye open would be a prudent precaution. The demarcation lines between the activities of the British Secret Service, Fine Gael, and sections of Fianna Fáil were very difficult to chart. I did not find any concrete evidence which would prove that they worked as a co-ordinated unit together. Rather I would say they moved on parallel lines having the same end result in view, namely, the political destruction of Charlie Haughey, and they did not damage each other. Nevertheless their stance in relation to many things, particularly the North, was much the same. Desmond Fennell's penetrating remarks are relevant here:

> Choose your stance. If you want the North to continue lurching from one horror to the next, ignore the injustice being done to the 600,000 Irish there. When you list the 'social injustices in present-day Ireland' leave that out. Get worked up about El Salvador, or the travelling people, or apartheid in South Africa, or the lack of crèche facilities in your district. Condemn the IRA vigorously. Cheer Dr FitzGerald when he says nice things about Britain, and be shocked by Mr Haughey when he makes angry, militant noises. That way, for sure, you'll get another fifteen years of it.

These words might usefully be framed and put on any journalist's desk.

In the event Haughey won the last battle. He won, because apart from being head and shoulders above any of his opponents, he had the grass roots of the Irish people behind him in the same way as Michael Collins had in the Black-and-Tan war, and De Valera in the Economic War. Hundreds of years of experience of the British media had taught those ordinary people to be wary. They did not have to reject all of what they were told but they prudently rejected perhaps fifty per cent of it.

One would have hoped and expected that this humiliating defeat for the media might have taught them a lesson. Indeed for many it did, but the recent removal of the whip from Desmond O'Malley by the Fianna Fáil parliamentary party might lead one to believe that many others did not grasp the lesson to be learned.

The facts of the case were very simple. O'Malley took upon himself the right to speak publicly on the sensitive issue of Northern Ireland in a way which seemed to contradict party policy as expressed by Haughey, as leader of the party. Haughey called a meeting of the parliamentary party and after a full debate the party unanimously decided that the leader of the party only, or someone designated by him, should be the one to speak for the party on such a sensitive issue. Since the vote was unanimous O'Malley must have voted in agreement. Yet almost immediately afterwards he spoke again publicly on Northern Ireland. Very correctly Haughey called another meeting of the parliamentary party and by a substantial majority the party voted to remove the whip from Mr O'Malley.

In itself this is not a matter of earth-shaking importance. It has happened before and no doubt it will happen again. But what is of considerable importance is how the media reacted. Columns upon columns of newspaper space and hours of radio and television time was given to this relatively trifling matter. Haughey was again the target. He was a dictator, an autocrat, an avenger. They forgot that in the past in other situations when he should have taken strong action and did not, they had described him as a weakling, spineless and even cowardly. A stranger in Ireland reading the screaming headlines in the newspapers might be forgiven for thinking that Ireland was in crisis and on the verge of a revolution. According to the media the shock waves vibrating throughout the country were such that the party was split asunder, a new onslaught on Haughey's leadership was imminent, there were going to be massive resignations and defections, etc. etc.

All this, of course, was a load of codswallop and nonsense. There were no shock waves whatever throughout the party. Out of 3,000 cumainn chairmen only three or four could be got to speak out against Haughey. At least ninety-eight per cent of the party supported him and party discipline, and the public at large treated the whole thing with quiet detached amusement. On the other hand, some of the more outstanding journalists judged the situation accurately and gave some balanced assessments of the situation pointing out that De Valera, Lemass, Jack Lynch, Liam Cosgrave, Garret FitzGerald had, in the past, gone much further than Haughey in their insistence on discipline and had formulated policies with scant consultation with the rank and file. Indeed in 1932 the Fianna Fáil party agreed that all announcements on national policy would be made by De Valera. It surely makes sense that on such a senstive issue, every TD should not be allowed to blow his top off when he feels in the mood to do so, especially on Northern Ireland matters where a lot of human lives may be at stake.

But like the wounded stag in the forest being snarled at by lesser animals, Haughey was there to be hammered, much to the delight of the British.

Writing recently in the *Sunday Press* Proinsias Mac Aonghusa said:

Not enough research has been carried out in Ireland to indicated how much trust people have in the media. But it is a fact that when all the papers and the broadcasting service act as one in presenting one side of a political or national affair as 'Right,' cynicism in the streets is great.

I think what happened in a number of cases was that some journalists accepted the OPERATION BROGUE line that Haughey was evil, and they falsely saw proof of this in his actions, where in fact there was no real proof in the first instance.

Yet in spite of all this I believe there is a change coming. More and more journalists are now prepared to admit privately that, as far as Haughey is concerned, they got it all wrong in the past. Even throughout the entire witch-hunt there were a number of perceptive journalists who wrote and spoke the truth and were not misled by British whisperings or OPERATION BROGUE. More and more are joining their ranks and are coming to realise that, where the British are concerned, there are no such things as free parties, free lunches, free drinks or free trips. Payment will be collected in due course.

There is an old Irish proverb which says *Fillean an feall ar an bhfeallaire* (the evil deed comes back on the doer) and it seems as if many elements within Fine Gael are beginning to learn this to their cost, as they are beginning to learn that crudeness and personal vilification do not pay off. If they want to defeat Charles Haughey they can try to do so, not by bubbly slogans or abuse, but by showing the Irish people in real practical terms that they have a superior policy and a superior leadership.

This lesson is a healthy one which the media should mark well. Ireland is their home, their country, whose freedom has been won at a terrible price. Like all of us they should play their part in serving it to the best of their ability. This they can do by following the guidelines laid down by the National Union of Journalists and by remembering that the lives and destiny of thousands of Irish people may very well depend upon their dedication to truth, freedom and justice and to the public's right to know *both* sides of the news. As I have already said that is 'Freedom of the Press'. In this way they can give the lie to Adlai Stevenson's quip that editors are men who separate the wheat from the chaff and then publish the chaff; and to John Osborne's quip that television is a medium run by dim untalented little bigots.

So the most balanced answer to the vital 'why' we posed at the beginning of the chapter is:

1. We cannot rule out the possibility that the British Secret Service has infiltrated important branches of the media.

2. It seems most likely that large sections of the media had the wool pulled over their eyes without their knowing so.

I have not yet enough hard evidence to go further than that.

7. The Leadership of Charles Haughey

We need men who can dream of things that never were, and ask why not.
                                                        – G. B. SHAW

Whoever takes up the sword shall perish by the sword.
And whoever does not take up the sword, or lets it go,
                    shall perish on the cross.
                                                        – SIMONE WEIL

There is a famine abroad – a famine not of bread nor of gold,
but a famine of really great men. We are starved with mediocrity,
we are dying of ordinariness, we are perishing of pettiness.
                                                        – FATHER MacDYER

Overlooking the square in the town of Arles in Provence, France, there is a prominent notice which reads:

TOURIST, you are in famous Provence, a country colonised, polluted and despoiled; its language forgotten, its ancient traditions betrayed, its soul extinguished.

Here is a town disgusted with central government, telling the truth about itself. No wonder it is thronged with visitors. It does not seem unreasonable to suggest that after sixty years of Dublin government, most towns in Ireland could truthfully display the same notice in their market squares.

I imagine that thinking Irishmen and women would accept that we have reached probably one of the lowest points in national morale since the post-Famine years.

Not only have we lost our native language with all its deep and inspirational connotations but two of our political parties go out of their way to insult and humiliate it. Our security forces are gradually becoming mere off-shoots of the British security forces, who cross our frontiers, land and sea, whenever they wish, seemingly with the tacit toleration of our government. We have let down the Nationalists of the North by giving them a false hope for sixty years and now when, thanks to our betrayal, they have taken the law into their own hands, we call them terrorists.

Our jails are full of these young Irishmen whose crime has been to challenge in arms the British forces who are brutalising their families and homes, while these same jails are empty of the real criminals who roam free to destroy our youth with drugs, and to murder our aged for a few pounds of their pension money.

We are now approaching the unprecedented unemployment figure of 250,000 while at the same time our shops are full of foreign vegetables which could be produced here and foreign goods which could be manufactured here. We are spending millions of pounds on 'jobs for the boys' and bizarre foreign junkets with first-class travel and luxury hotels. There is a mood of despair permeating every facet of Irish life. We are suffering from a paralysis of greed handed down by our politicians, many of whom have lost any ideals they had. Do they give a damn about Ireland?

When Garret FitzGerald took over Fine Gael his speeches instilled hope of a renewed Ireland where government of the nod, the wink and the nudge would be a thing of the past. I was one of those who believed those high sounding words, only to find, like so many thousands of others, that when his government came to power almost their first act was to spend hundreds of thousands of pounds of our money in giving jobs to party supporters many of whom had little or no qualifications for these jobs. Since then scarcely a month passes that some party supporter is not given a plum job. This was a bitter disappointment. It looked as if the new Ireland was little more than an election gimmick. 'Never judge a man by what he says – only by what he does' is a maxim as old as human nature yet we forget it at every election.

It is not within the scope of this book to examine in detail this depressing narrative which must make the survivors of our freedom struggle wonder if their comrades, so brutally done to death, had given their lives for nothing. It is only pertinent here to touch on this subject in so far as it will strike Mr Haughey head on when he assumes leadership of a new government.

In writing this chapter I am conscious of the quip that the secrets of success are known only to those who have not succeeded. I must admit I have not even tried. I have never been a member of any political party so it is only as an interested observer of history and politics that I write.

Whenever I attend a social function there is usually someone who approaches me with free advice as to how I can write and publish better books. Most of what I listen to is pure rubbish but very often there comes some idea or proposal that is of very real value. It is in this spirit that I make a number of suggestions I know will be greeted by many with alarm and dismay, and will undoubtedly shock some readers who have been lulled into a state of mental stupor by the daily diet of slanted news.

Comparisons sometimes help. In one sense the task facing Haughey is almost as great as that which faced Konrad Adenauer when he began the labours of rebuilding Germany after the Second World War. In another sense it is even more formidable. Adenauer was faced with a country literally in ruins, burdened with an intolerable public debt in the form of reparations; a country partitioned by victorious powers and the partitioned part held by force and violence; and an opposition party spiritually aligned with the occupying power.

The parallel with Ireland is clear. Haughey will be faced by ruins, not as numerous as in Germany, but ruins all the same; the ruins of hundreds of empty factories, and hundreds more of small businesses, destroyed by politicians who were really unable to run a country and by civil servants who pontificated nonsense from their armchairs. Haughey will be faced by a public debt higher per capita than that of Germany. He will, like Adenauer, have to face a country partitioned by victorious armies, and the partitioned parts held by force and violence, with courts of justice and police every bit as sinister as those behind the iron curtain. Perhaps worst of all, he will be faced by an active opposition party, spiritually aligned with the occupying power and more often than not ready to make obeisance to that power and do its bidding. Yet Adenauer built Germany into one of the greatest and most prosperous countries in western Europe. Can Haughey do the same?

Adenauer had one great advantage over Haughey. He had behind him a nation who believed in their native land and culture and who were willing to work and make sacrifices for the future of their people; in other words, a people who had not lost their soul; a political party, the then CDU, behind him, who were men and women of vision and idealism, whose primary task was to rebuild the nation and not to feather their own nests; and perhaps of equal importance, and so unlike Ireland, a nation unwilling to collaborate in any way with the power occupying the partitioned part of their land. He was a leader with the qualities of finely tempered steel. He never toadyed to or boot-licked the Russians. He never collaborated with the security forces of the partitioned part of this country. He never extradited his own people to a criminal regime. It was he who made the profound remark: 'An infallible method of conciliating a tiger is to allow oneself to be devoured' – a comment which Irish politicians should mark well.

Unfortunately it is true that Haughey will have to start from a point much lower than Adenauer. He will have to resurrect in the Irish people an idealism which they have lost, and a sense of identity which years of toadyism and subserviant political leadership has eroded and he will have to make them feel once again proud of their Irishness. He will have to bring a dead nation to life. That will be the hardest, by far, of his tasks.

This will call for a degree of personal idealism such as we have not seen since the early years of the state. The government of the nod, the wink, the fix, the jobs-for-the-boys, the over-pandering to the vote, the incompetence, the toadyism will have to change and government by ability and integrity will have to begin. Of course it will not be all that perfect. Government by Tammany Hall methods is as old as man himself and it would be foolish to think it can be eliminated altogether, but it can be brought to manageable proportions.

For more than forty years I have closely observed Irish politics and I have never known the Irish people to display a degree of cynicism such as they display at the moment. In their eyes the majority of politicians are both dishonest and incompetent, interested only in personal advantage and prepared to exploit every situation, however tragic, in the hope of getting extra votes to further their own interests. The unemployment, the dole queues, those on the bread line were all put to one side while the art of mud-slinging was brought to the centre of the stage. It is that kind of government which must be brought to an end.

Everything is now up for sale if it can produce more votes: our freedom, our constitution, our national territory, our language, our culture and even our greatest asset, the youth of our country. Only the acquisition of votes is now sacred. This seems a harsh judgement but as Goethe said: 'The people may often be wrong on details but they are usually right on the whole.'

While our country is being ruled predominantly from London and Brussels and only marginally from Dublin, with nearly a quarter of a million unemployed, with a crisis of confidence in our fundamental institutions such as our judiciary, our police and our code of justice, with our statute books bursting at the seams with repressive legislation – we have more than any other country in Western Europe – with despair facing our young people, one cannot rule out the possibility that we are sitting on a time bomb that could one day explode into a terrible civil war. In this light one can see the enormity of the task facing Charles Haughey when he next comes to power. How should he tackle it?

It this chapter I take the bit between my teeth and suggest a number of ideas – ideas which in view of the present sad state of affairs, should be given reasonable consideration and not be rejected out of hand. They are not the views of an experienced politician or a revisionist historian but the views of an outsider who cares about his country and his people and who feels that their days of leadership by incompetence and toadyism should now be brought to a close.

I believe he will have to start by reforming the Fianna Fáil party itself. Fianna Fáil was once a great party; a party that spoke for the ordinary people, a party that was founded to promulgate the noblest of ideals, the freedom of our country, the restoration of our language and culture, the ownership of the wealth of the country by the people, in other words, the ideals of Davis, Tone and Pearse. How the party degenerated is not part of this book. It is told effectively in Kevin Boland's *The Rise and Decline of Fianna Fáil.* It makes sad reading.

Fianna Fáil probably reached its lowest ebb in 1969/70 when it turned its back on the people of the North and used the army and police force to help the British further crush fellow Irishmen.

In school we were taught that the great betrayal in Irish history was the Act of Union. I do not think that this is valid. The Act of Union betrayed only about one per cent of the people – the Anglo-Irish living around Dublin – the Dublin 4 set of today – the other ninety-nine per cent, living in slavery, hardly knew it happened. It could very well be that future generations will see 1969/70 as the greatest betrayal in all Irish history. It will be one of the hardest parts of Haughey's task to reverse that betrayal, to restore the confidence of the people of the North and to try and salvage all he can from the shattered remains of Fianna Fáil ideals. This may be the very first step in reducing violence.

He will have to begin by nailing his colours to the mast and re-stating Fianna Fáil's policy as De Valera did in 1926. Here I am reminded of an incident in the life of the great English historian and writer, Hilaire Belloc. When Belloc was about to address his first public meeting in his campaign to be elected Liberal MP for Salford, his campaign manager, Sir Edward Wood, all his advisers, and even the clergy warned him not to make any references to the fact that he was a Catholic since this could have a disastrous effect on his chances by alienating the predominantly Protestant vote. Belloc stood up and addressed the packed meeting:

> Gentlemen, I am a Catholic. As far as possible I go to Mass every day. This (taking a Rosary beads from his pocket) is a Rosary. As far as possible I kneel down and tell these beads every day. If you reject me on account of my religion I shall thank God he has spared me the indignity of being your representative.

There was a stunned silence for a moment. Then there was a roar of deafening applause. Belloc was elected.

Perhaps I may be forgiven for indulging in a bit of hypothesis if I suggest that Mr Haughey should face the Irish public and say:

> I am an Irishman. I believe passionately in the unity and freedom of my country. I am not going to collaborate in any way with the occupying power. I am going to take every step necessary to free my people from the bondage they suffer under. I shall not rest until I see an independent, free Thirty-two County Irish Republic. If you reject me for this reason then do so. I shall then thank God I have been spared the indignity of representing you, for you are not worth it!

If he spoke like that, I believe the people would sweep him into power and keep him there. The great leaders like De Valera, De Gaulle, Adenauer, Gasperi and Lincoln were not ashamed of the ideals of liberty they stood for and the people trusted them. The Irish are now sick of mediocrity and shiftiness in their leaders.

Not the least important task facing Mr Haughey will be the removal of any members of the party whose home is really with Fine Gael. Here he will simply have to be ruthless and remember the telling words of the late Marquis of Halifax: 'State business is a cruel trade; good nature is a bungler in it.' To allow considerations of unity within the party to influence his dealings with these people would be a mistake. There will never be unity while many of them are there and in the composition of a cabinet they should be ruthlessly excluded, unless they are prepared to give unqualified loyalty to the leader and to the Republican ideals of the party. In choosing his cabinet De Valera sought loyalty above everything else. If they are given cabinet responsibility on any other conditions they could wait until their public prestige has been built up to a point where they could make demands under threat of resignation. In the interests of party unity Haughey extended the hand of friendship to George Colley and others only to have it spurned and a lot of later troubles arose from a lack of ruthlessness here. That is a lesson which he should mark well. The task now to be attempted is so great that absolute unity and discipline within the party is essential. Nothing short of the type of unity De Valera was able to count on in 1932 will meet the needs of the present day.

As a gesture of courage, and even honourable defiance, he should invite back into the party men like Kevin Boland and Neil Blaney and in that way try and heal the past, rather than being soft on others who will knife him metaphorically if they get the chance. At least Boland and Blaney will not do that.

The restoration, not only to the party but to the front bench, of Seán Doherty, would be telling the British elements in the country, loud and clear, that he spurns their lying propaganda and sees through it for what it is and that he accepts Seán Doherty, as those who worked under him and with him accept, as a capable, efficient minister.

Another area where the most drastic and radical decisions

may have to be taken is in our relationship with Great Britain. To discuss our relationship with Britain naturally raises a very penetrating question: *What is Britain's track record in her past relationship with Ireland?* Sadly enough this is a question which any school-child can answer without having to think.

It is a record of which no nation could be proud. A record of hundreds of years of plunder and destruction where millions of our kinsmen were slaughtered and countless thousands of our young children were sold as slaves to the West Indies. Famines were promoted on such a scale as to convince one that it was a deliberate policy of genocide.

It would be a pleasant task to record that all that is over and gone and belongs to past history. Unfortunately such is not the case. On a more modified scale, as these lines are being written, the same murder, torture, brutality is continuing in Northern Ireland with no let up. As I have already said Britain needs that part of our country for military purposes and she will continue with her brutality irrespective of how many Irish lives are lost. The leopard does not readily change its spots and I do not think I am being wildly alarmist if I suggest that if Britain could get away with taking the South by force she would do so and presumably each and every one of us could expect the same medicine as that being meted out to our fellow countrymen in the North. With history constantly repeating itself it would therefore be a most foolish politician indeed who would ignore this track record because what the people of the North are suffering today, we could be suffering tomorrow. The tyrannies of Hitler were too obvious – that is what led to his downfall. The British tyranny, while exactly the same, is not so obvious – that is why it succeeds.

As I was putting the final touches to this book (September 1984) the newspapers announced that there was a likelihood of some new initiative on Northern Ireland. It appears that instead of throwing a few crumbs to us, Margaret Thatcher is now going to throw us a crust. The delight with which this new insult will be received remains to be seen. Even if the British were to say that they will leave Ireland in five or ten years time, they cannot be trusted. 'The history of Ireland,' De Valera once remarked, 'is a history of broken treaties.' Such a declaration would be hedged with so many conditions as to render it worthless. It would simply be a ploy to boost the Coalition and to wrench

more and more policing from us, and to have more and more
Irishmen extradited. Will we never learn? Will we never stop
fooling ourselves?

Another *realpolitik* factor in relationship with Britain is something which should be obvious to everyone: *Britain in her long
history has only yielded to force.* Freedom, justice, human rights
have never had a role in any occupied territory. We have only
to look at Cyprus, Palestine, Aden, Egypt, Kenya, etc. to prove
that statement. They have left a trail of blood everywhere behind
them. In view of this track record could any reasonable person
have confidence that she will return Northern Ireland without
force?

De Valera never rejected the principle of force. He simply
did not believe it would work. But early in the war he told the
American Ambassador, John Cudahy, that if he had at his disposal an army as strong as Germany he 'would move on the
North and settle partition conclusively.'

I do not want my readers to think I am advocating the use of
force in the sense of bullets and bombs. If I thought they would
succeed I would not hesitate to do so since a nation is fully
entitled to take all steps to rid its territory of an invader. As
Margaret Thatcher so rightly said:

> You have to be prepared to defend the things in which you believe
> and be prepared to use force to secure the furture of liberty and
> self-determination.

And again, Michael Collins said:

> While England explains the futility of force by others it is the only
> argument she listens to.

But there is such a thing as 'soft force' which I think could be
used with great effect. What I mean by 'soft force' is every form
of pressure, embarrassment, vexation, constraint, scourge,
which will hurt Britain in every way possible, particularly in her
pocket and in the field of world opinion. 'The world is ruled by
force,' says Pascal, 'but opinion uses force.' And D. P. Moran
reminds us that 'England has no sentiment that will not go under
before the gentlest tap of self-interest.'

The big focal point where British and Irish interests overlap is, of course, Northern Ireland. People in the South know very little of what is happening there. It has been carefully concealed from them and they have been subjected to catch phrases which are totally false.

One of the great catch-phrases of British propaganda is that in Ireland there are two nations. There are not two nations. There is one nation only, with different traditions. There are, of course, two traditions in the North, but there are *three* traditions in the South, the Gaelic, the Irish and the Anglo-Irish. In Switzerland, Belgium, France, the United States and other countries there are several traditions. The existence of different traditions does not mean that each tradition must have its own political independence. In all these countries the various traditions are able to live and work in harmony, but the desire of one tradition to be overlord and to have all the goodies and to use violence, brutality and murder to hold them is the reason the two traditions in Northern Ireland cannot work together. It is foolish and naïve to believe in the catch-phrase that the Unionist can be wooed into joining a United Ireland. Since the foundations of their statelet the British gave them virtually everything they wanted. With fifty-five per cent of the population they had ninety per cent of all employment in government services. One cabinet minister, Sir Dawson Bates, had such a hatred of Nationalists that not even the most junior clerk in his ministry was to be employed if he were a Catholic. In one purge Sir Basil Brooke sacked one hundred and twenty-five employees when he found out they were Catholics. His exact words were: 'If we in Ulster allow Roman Catholics to work on our farms we are traitors to Ulster.' They have full control of the police which is almost entirely Unionist and since its formation has operated with a brutal efficiency which many have compared to the Gestapo or South African police. Some time ago a question in the House of Commons produced the following information: in 1971 there were 17,291 raids on Catholic homes. In 1972 this had risen to 36,614 and in 1974 had risen again to 71,914. *This is approximately two hundred houses raided per day.* I have witnessed some of these raids and they are not a pleasant sight; men, women and children dragged out of their beds screaming, kicked and beaten up, furniture, pictures and family heirlooms smashed and in some cases the raiders have been known to urinate in the hallways when leaving. According to an article in the *Irish Times* Father Denis Faul made 1,500 complaints to the British government about the conduct of the security forces not one of which was dealt with. Again the Unionists have almost complete control of the courts where a majority of judges are so bigoted that a Catholic or Nationalist stands little chance of justice.

These people have been in charge of the state since it was founded and have had all the goodies. There is no way whatever by which they can be enticed into a United Ireland because they would have to share their goodies democratically, and any Irish politician who says they can is either dishonest or living in cloud-cuckoo land. Perhaps the most brilliant and truthful summary of conditions in the North was given in a recent lecture by Bernadette McAliskey:

> When we started out demanding civil rights, equal opportunity to vote, to employment and to a roof over our heads we had no idea that we were going to end up in the position we are in today. But we got there by a very logical political process. . . In the beginning people said we ought to do things within the law. We didn't have a natural aversion to the law, but every time we looked like winning anything they changed it. What was legal yesterday became illegal today. We started exercising the freedoms we had within the law, but we found that if we used them effectively, they were translated into behaviour 'likely to lead to a breach of the peace'.
>
> You are allowed freedom of organisation if you don't use it. You are allowed freedom of speech if you use it to back up the existing order and administration. But if you use freedom of speech to say 'I don't think the system works' that is no longer freedom of speech, that is incitement. That is behaviour likely to cause a breach of the peace, and to get your head smashed in by a police-man. . .
>
> They told us to use the democratic process and we used it. We used it way back in 1918, we used it when Bobby Sands was dying and Sinn Féin have used it since. But there is a problem with the democratic process. If you elect people which the government think are not suitable, they scurry like rats into the House of Commons and pass a law saying you are allowed to elect people of your choice as long as you do not elect people of the following calibre. If you

elect those people then we will pretend that you didn't. . .

Politically they have taken away all our rights so that we stand on the wrong side of the law. They introduced the Diplock courts without juries and six thousand people in Northern Ireland passed through them in ten years – something like one in every hundred people.

We have a problem with operating within the law, not simply because they change it all the time, but because they have now taken their politics right into the courts. . . We were born guilty.

We are part of an Irish community who were historically forced to live within a state whose legality and whose right to exist we have never ever conceded. *We live in a country where all that is brave, good, idealistic and hopeful is in gaol. All that is underhand, petty, mean and dishonest is in power.* (Italics mine)

These are frightening words, but even more frightening is the way we have co-operated with the British to break these noble people. We have betrayed them, even though we claim them constitutionally. Our answer to their cries for help has been to side with their oppressors. 'Please don't bother us,' we have said. 'Please shut up. Let us enjoy our oysters, our caviar, our champagne and our smoked salmon.'

We now come to a major *realpolitik* question which has to be looked at in any assessment of Mr Haughey's role as a leader of the future Ireland. We spend over two hundred and fifty million pounds a year protecting the border for the British. Old men and women in our major cities are robbed daily and beaten – sometimes to death – for a few pounds because there are no gardaí to protect them – they are away protecting the border. Our young children and teenagers are being corrupted on an alarming scale through the use of drugs, again because the police who could prevent this are away protecting the border. Common criminals who are sentenced by our courts to long terms of imprisonment are released after a few months or a few weeks so that there will be room in our prisons for those whom the British demand we keep there. It is no longer safe for man, woman or child to walk the streets of our cities or the roads of our countryside – there are no police to protect them. Every whim of the British is satisfied no matter what it costs. It is estimated that it cost over £200,000 to pursue and catch Dominic McGlinchey. What could be done with all that kind of money if it were diverted to the safety of the poor and the old?

Small shopkeepers in our cities, particularly in Dublin, trying to make a living in the face of heavy taxation, have now an added burden – protection money. Many of them are being forced to pay between £50 and £100 weekly to gangs of criminals and there are not adequate police available to investigate or catch these criminals. They are largely occupied chasing the innocent men who escaped from Long Kesh concentration camp while the whole fabric of law and order on the social level, is falling down around them.

When one poses the question: How can any self-respecting people allow that, one is reluctantly forced to the conclusion that we have been and are being led by weak, incompetent and inept politicians. It is wrong to assume that because a man is elected to parliament he is *ipso facto* a capable leader. If he is, then it is purely accidental. 'Nations would be terrified,' remarked General de Gaulle, 'if they knew by what small men they are ruled.' I do not think that in Ireland we have given sufficient thought to the notion of incompetence in our leaders. In the matter of subserviance to the British we are inclined to call them traitors and puppets. This is unfair. Many of them were simply incompetent men unequal to the job, who were unable to see how the British fooled them and walked rings around them. In an earlier chapter I have shown how the highly competent and professional British got almost every concession they demanded, while at the same time not giving one iota to our leaders. Perhaps the best way to look at this question is to imagine that you have won one million pounds and you want to invest it wisely and productively. Would you entrust this money to any of our top political leaders today? That is *realpolitik* question. We have had more than our share of duds.

A further suspicion is somewhat more alarming. There is a considerable body of opinion, especially among young people, who strongly suspect that a large majority of our political leaders do *not* want a united Ireland. They argue as follows: if we had a united Ireland we would have at least fifty TDs from the North of which thirty would be Unionists. If they held the balance of power they could create havoc by demanding cabinet posts, and their share of 'jobs-for-the-boys'. Many of our ministers whose benefits, salaries and perks come to over £100,000 per annum, might not be too anxious to lose all that by overworking themselves for a united Ireland. 'It is difficult,' says the writer Upton Sinclair, 'to get a man to understand something when his salary depends on his not understanding it.' So when a politician says 'I want a united Ireland but only with the consent of the Unionists and by peaceful means,' then that is seen by many young people as pure rubbish and is being translated into *real-politik* English as saying: 'I really don't want a United Ireland because I could lose my lucrative perks, money and power. So lest I lose votes I will say I want a united Ireland but only by consent. This I know will never happen, but by saying so I protect my own financial interests and my votes.' This attitude may well be called cynicism, but is it? Or is it truth? I suggest that you just pause and think about it.

In bringing Ireland back to nationhood Mr Haughey will have to make an unequivocal statement to the public, such as that made by De Valera in 1926, to the effect that the Six Counties are part of the nation and it will have them back – a statement as unconditional as it is clear.

I also think he will have to go even further than that and publicly admit that Fianna Fáil's role as collaborator with the British from 1969/70 onwards *was a grave mistake and was not consistent with the purposes for which the organisation was founded.*

The Fianna Fáil Cabinet issued a statement early on in the Troubles which said: 'The employment of British troops is unacceptable and not likely to restore peaceful conditions.' Why then collaborate with this army if it is unacceptable? The British have said: 'The Six Counties are ours. Let us torture our citizens in peace.' We must reply loud and clear for all the world to hear: 'They are not yours and we will not let you torture our people in peace.'

Such policies imply the immediate rectifying of the legislative mistakes made by Fianna Fáil, such as the revoking of section 31 of the Broadcasting Act, which is an insult to the intelligence of the Irish people, the tightening up of the Extradition Act to ensure that *no* Irishmen are ever extradited to the Castlereagh torture chambers or the Diplock show trials, an *immediate halt to all collaboration between the gardaí and Northern security forces* and an amnesty for all political prisoners held in our jails.

There are many in Irish politics today who have forgotten the words of Seán T. O'Kelly relative to the political prisoners jailed by W. T. Cosgrave in Arbour Hill: 'I would not condemn the prisoners in Arbour Hill who believe in gun violence.'

No doubt this will cause a great outcry. Fine Gael, Labour, the British and the media will unite to try to destroy him once again. But the people will support a man of such greatness. They did it before. De Valera released all the political prisoners when he came to power in 1932. The outcry was loud and shrill. Fine Gael posters and advertisements said:

> THE GUNMEN ARE VOTING FIANNA FÁIL.
> HOW WILL YOU VOTE?
> and
> A VOTE FOR FIANNA FÁIL IS A VOTE FOR
> THE RELEASE OF TERRORISTS.

What a familiar ring! He was attacked by Fine Gael, the British and the media. He was they said, ruining the country, bringing it to the verge of civil war, destroying for ever Anglo-Irish relations, a breaker of treaties, a madman. But what happened? The people stood with him and he won election after election, and soon the British saw that they were dealing with a man of steel, and in the end they swallowed their pride, dumped Fine Gael, and made peace with De Valera. The people will always follow a leader of greatness. Some will say 'You can't treat the British like that. We are economically dependent on them.' That is a spurious argument. We were much more economically dependent on them in 1932 when we took them on and won. Will that leader be Charles J. Haughey?

It may very well be if he publicly declares:

1. Part of our country is forcibly occupied by an alien power which uses brutality to oppress and keep in subjection the minority.

2. That the occupying British have no intention of ending their occupation unless strong pressure of some form or another is used.

3. That no Fianna Fáil government can ever collaborate in any way with security forces such as are in control in Northern Ireland.

4. That whether there is loss of ministerial salaries and perks, or whatever the financial consequences to individuals, the unity of the country comes first.

I believe if he states these policies, loud and clear, the people will follow him. They are weary of equivocation, verbal dissimulation and pretence. They now need the sincerity and strength of real leadership.

A further element in the earlier Fianna Fáil policies which Mr Haughey may have to revitalise is their approach to the Irish language. This again will have to be radical. On one occasion in the twenties when the old Fine Gael government were short of money they gave serious consideration to selling our most precious national monument, the GPO. It was as if every element of nationalism was up for sale. Later in Coalition they sold the Irish language in the hope of winning a few extra votes, by making Ireland the only country in the world whose native language is not mandatory in the educational system. This I believe will need to be reversed and compulsory Irish again introduced thus bringing us back once again into the main stream of European culture and thought, and removing us from the cultural cesspool in which we are. The practical details of how this should be done would take an entire volume in itself, but a beginning might be made while still in opposition by countering tooth and nail the ignorant and insulting approach of the Coalition parties towards the language. Other countries have revived their language. Czechoslovakia revived its two languages, Czech and Slovak, when they were in a much worse condition than Ireland, when its people spoke German as we do English, and when the revival was opposed for the identical reasons Irish is opposed today. When Czechoslovakia became a free country in 1918 it was said that competent speakers of the languages could be accommodated in one large room. Yet now they are the day-to-day language of seven million people. Hungary, Rumania, Bulgaria, Greece and Finland all revived their languages within half a century. But not Ireland.

Closely allied to the question of the language is the question of our system of education. We need only ask ourselves that if Pearse were to write today his devastating attack on the British educational system in Ireland in his book *The Murder Machine* would he have to change much of it? The answer is, of course, that it could almost stand as it is without change. Here is an area again needing drastic and painful change.

The area of Foreign Affairs is one where we have reached a very low point in national morale. Many of our embassies abroad are mere ventriloquists' dummies for the British embassies – they must wait to hear what the British line is first. For more than ten years now most of them have consistently supported British policy on the North, and few if any, have ever attempted to oppose that line. Our embassies abroad should mirror our people, our culture, our belief in freedom and the justice of our cause, to the countries where they are accredited. If I posed the question: are they doing that? the answer would be most likely a burst of derisory laughter! More than any other department of state this is the one that has let down the Irish people significantly. It has been little more than the hind tit of the British diplomatic service. Indeed Nobel-prizewinner, Mr Séan Mac-Bride, has publicly accused some civil servants in the Department of Foreign Affairs, of actively working to bring us into NATO and to end our neutrality.

Perhaps the most painful and far-reaching change of direction which Mr Haughey will have to look at is that of the Common Market itself. With our industries almost destroyed, our agriculture in chaos, our farmers on the verge of bankruptcy, our unemployment approaching a quarter of a million, most reasonable people now accept that our entry into this association was a major political blunder. We were simply misled by our leaders whose competence must surely come into question. The EEC has been a failure as far as Ireland is concerned. European countries such as Switzerland and Austria, who stayed out of the EEC, fared much better. Before it is too late we should withdraw, and substitute a series of external trading agreements like other countries. This will be another hard decision. If Haughey takes it he may expect massive attacks from the minority who are making small personal fortunes from the EEC gravy train. Since many of these are closely linked with the media he may expect massive attacks from there also. But he survived them before and he can do so again.

Another element in the life of the nation crying out for change is our whole approach to work. We are now in the ludicrous position that in the majority of cases it is more profitable to go on the dole than to work. This is having a terrible effect on those who do actually work. They see their colleagues idling and at the same time taking home more pay than if they were working. We should quickly be made to accept the principle that no dole or social welfare should be paid for idleness. Unemployment benefit is made necessary by the uncertainties of a modern state but it should only be paid out for work. What I mean is that people on the dole should be obliged to do at least four hours community work per day. Community work would entail keeping towns, villages, parks tidy; helping with limited area afforestation, involvement in community projects such as helping the aged, involvement in youth work. Farmers on the dole should be obliged to cultivate portion of their holdings for the benefit of the poor and the sick. I found out lately that the amount of dole paid in the Shannon watershed area would be sufficient to capitalise the whole river drainage scheme, which would save hundreds of thousands of acres of farm land and benefit the farmers to the extent of millions of pounds.

Is there any reason why young school leavers should not be compelled to spend a year in the defence forces before qualifying for social welfare? Army life would do them a lot of good and perhaps they could be used to help the police in patrolling high crime density areas in our cities.

Closely allied to the question of work is the question of industrial relations. Ours must surely be one of the worst in the world with one strike after another for such things as travel money, danger money, dirt money, disturbance money, etc. We have the most wasteful system of restrictive practices in Europe where large sections of the workforce receive salaries for doing absolutely nothing.

The list is almost endless. The outlawing completely of unofficial strikes, not by jailing the participants but by depriving them of any social welfare, is something that ought to be looked at closely. In voting for strike action, would a 'family vote' not be the most sensible method? i.e. a married man or woman would have two votes, a married man or woman with one child would have three votes and so on. This would eliminate a large number of irresponsible strikes.

If we ask why such commonsense ideas are not put to use, we turn up the old sickening question of votes. Politicians will not implement them because they are afraid of losing votes. They will give scores of empty excuses using the word 'democracy' but the 'almighty vote' is at the back of it all.

Now I would like to suggest that such is not the case. I believe a capable and decisive leader who would implement such ideas would actually *increase* his share of the vote. The public are sick and tired of paying enormous taxes to support irresponsible doles, ludicrous restrictive practices and wild-cat strikes. In a last analysis somebody must pay for this terrible inefficiency and that somebody is the ordinary working member of the public. The leadership that would take us out of this mess would get massive public support as well as massive support from those on the dole because everyone would see that the country had at last a leader who was going to lead them out of the terrible muddle they are now in and that any sacrifices called for would only be temporary. The most important single element in business is good management and in the affairs of a nation, good leadership. In their absence both businesses and nations die.

I have many times referred to the role played by the British Secret Service in Ireland and I fear that I have barely touched the tip of a massive iceberg. I have only been able to publish about twenty per cent of what I learned and I feel that a complete book on these abuses in Ireland is called for. I suspect that their operations are far more widespread than most people know and that these operations are targeted directly at such fundamental issues as our constitution and our whole existence as an independent state. Militarily Britain needs us very badly and the only way, short of direct invasion, she can be absolutely sure of having us is to control us as a satellite state. It does not seem unreasonable that she should spend vasts sums of money to bring that about, firstly by changing the climate of opinion in the country through clever propaganda, secondly by infiltrating every facet of Irish life, and thirdly by depressing us economically. I also believe that it was the role of the British Secret Service in bringing it about that Seán Doherty uncovered and was in the process of eradicating when there was a change of government. Doherty's lips are sealed by the Official Secrets Act and the only way we can now find out is by having a judicial inquiry, where the provisions of the Act would be put aside. The Coalition have refused such an inquiry.

If there is a reasonable chance that there is substance in what
I say, then these people are the real terrorists and far more
dangerous than any Republican paramilitaries. Indeed the
massive propaganda attacks on the paramilitaries may well be
the smoke screen to cover up much more sinister activities. We
now have strong evidence that it was the British Secret Service
who were responsible for several bombings and several bank
robberies carried out here in the South, with the object of dis-
crediting the IRA. There is also strong evidence to show that
they were responsible for a number of murders in border areas.
We all know of the activities of Crinnion and the Littlejohns
and indeed the suspected involvement of Christopher Ewart-
Biggs – but were they only the small fry? Are the big fish still
at large and working actively? I think they are. The recent revelations of Captain Fred Holroyd, former British Intelligence
Officer, in *The New Statesmen,* tell of kidnap plots, assassina-
tions, bombings and bank raids that are simply frightening.
There is one extremely serious allegation that the gardaí actually
co-operated in an attempt to kidnap Eamon McGurgan and
bring him over the border.

To counteract the devastating effect these people are having
on the nation, we should immediately establish a *Counter-Intelligence Organisation,* independent of the gardaí and Minister
for Justice and answerable directly to an all-party committee,
presided over by the Taoiseach. This organisation should not
be diverted by Republican activity but should concentrate on
tracking down and destroying the British spy system here before
it destroys us. There is already in existence in the gardaí a 'Red
Section' to carry out surveillance on the Russians, but no special
unit to watch the British, who are a far greater danger to the
state. This I believe will be a top priority task for Mr Haughey
when he returns to power.

Well, that ends my short piece of gratuitous advice as to where
drastic, painful decisions will have to be taken if we are to survive, or indeed to avoid a revolution or civil war. We have tried
the orthodox and it has failed. Let us now try the unorthodox.

To conclude, we should perhaps take a look at the personal
qualities of Charles J. Haughey and see how he is fitted for the

enormity of what lies before him.

Charles J. Haughey was born in Castlebar in September 1925. His father was an army officer who hailed from the North and his mother was also a Northerner. Both had good pre-Truce records. While still a young boy the family transferred to Dublin and having completed his secondary education, he took his degree in commerce in UCD. It was while he was a student at UCD that the first incident showing his Republicanism took place. The day the Second World War ended, in the ensuing euphoria amongst a small pro-British set in Dublin, the Union Jack was hoisted over Trinity College. Haughey was one of a group of Republican students who climbed the building and took it down.

While still a student he joined Fianna Fáil. Three years later he got to know Seán Lemass' daughter, Maureen, whom he married in 1948. He stood as a Fianna Fáil candidate in the following three elections and was defeated. There is no evidence here that his relationship with Seán Lemass was of any great help. Finally in 1957 he was elected to Dáil Éireann but it may well be that his election sowed seeds of bitterness which were to bear fruit in the distant future. The man he defeated was Harry Colley, father of George Colley.

In those early days there were other seeds sown which were also to have far-reaching results. Lemass encouraged young men of ability and promise to join the party and offer themselves for election. These were later disparagingly referred to as the 'mohair brigade', a reference to the well-cut clothes they wore, so unlike the homespun of earlier Fianna Fáil. It was unfortunate that many of these young men, though by no means all, had little in common with the roots of the party. They were indifferent to the unity of the country, the brutalities in the North, the fate of the Irish language. They were primarily interested in their own personal careers as politicians and would have been just as much at home in Fine Gael or Labour. They were, however, shrewd enough to see that joining Fianna Fáil was the best bet. The other two parties were sluggish, inert and lifeless, and Fianna Fáil was going places. It is interesting to note that in the seventies when Fianna Fáil had lost its soul and was rapidly declining very similar young 'mohair' men joined Fine Gael. It seems to be an inevitable law of political life that such groups will always be there, ready to jump into that party which offers them the most personal benefits.

But for Fianna Fáil the consequences have been most serious. It is a party based on ideals and ideals have no place in many of these people's eyes. If Haughey does not ruthlessly curb them he may well have major trouble on his hands in the future.

Haughey, about this time, started an accounting firm with some colleagues and over the years the firm prospered. This was subsequently held as a black mark against him. Seemingly his critics would have preferred it if he were a failure. The fact that he was a success through hard work, initiative and vision did not seem to merit praise.

His purchase of the tiny island of Innishvickalaun as a holiday retreat displeased certain elements who would see nothing wrong with him purchasing a retreat in France or Portugal, as some of his critics did – far from the eyes of the Irish media. On Innisvickalaun he built a small house from local materials and employed Irish labour to do the work. He does not own a helicopter. Very rarely he hires one of the local helicopters when some unusual circumstances comes about that warrants it. His supplies are landed by boat and hauled up a cliff by derrick. Here he holidays during the summer with his wife, Maureen, his children and their friends, and very occasionally a few guests. Perhaps had he used the government executive jet to go to the Mediterranean for his holidays he would come in for less criticism.

There are indeed many of his critics among the great Fianna Fáil and Fine Gael families who might usefully cast a glance at the origins of their own wealth and ascertain why it was all right for them to become wealthy and all wrong for Charlie Haughey. Why is it that in the eyes of some of the media due praise is given to people who become wealthy provided that their name is not Haughey?

Quite recently, in May 1984, the *Irish Press* reported that an estimated £750,000 was being paid for a tea and wholesale company owned by the family interests of Minister for Foreign Affairs, Mr Peter Barry, who is, incidentally, one of the most enlightened members of the Fine Gael party. Now all one can say is 'more power to them'. I wish to heaven some one would pay me a fraction of that sum for my small business interests. This matter was treated as an ordinary news item and it was dead the following day. But what would have happened if it were Charlie Haughey who sold part of his interests for £750,000? Would Dublin buzz with rumours? Would there be screaming headlines on all the newspapers for a week following? Would there be special radio and TV programmes? Would there be pompous comments about integrity in high places, etc.? These are hypothetical questions, but taking track records into account it is unlikely the matter would be dead and forgotten the following day.

When Haughey was three years in the Dáil Lemass began to take soundings in the party as to who might make a good parliamentary secretary to Oscar Traynor, Minister for Justice, who was ageing and unwell. Lemass was somewhat surprised to find the recurrance of the name Haughey in the recommendations of those he consulted. Traynor himself was in favour of Haughey. At a cabinet meeting he said to Lemass: 'Don't we all know the most suitable man is Charlie Haughey. The only thing against him is that he is your son-in-law and that should not be a consideration.' Lemass then offered him the job but said: 'As Taoiseach I am offering you this job on behalf of the government, but as your father-in-law I am advising you not to take it.' This was probably a hint that he would do better for himself and his family in accounting rather than politics. Haughey did not take the hint. Instead he took the job.

A year later when Oscar Traynor retired Haughey became Minister for Justice. Then began a career of ministerial brilliance which was only interrupted when Lynch sacked him in 1970. Peter Berry, Secretary of the Department of Justice, who was certainly no friend of Haughey, admitted on his retirement that of the fourteen ministers he had served under Haughey was the ablest. Indeed the exact words Berry used were 'dynamic and a joy to work with'. He began a course of law reform which not only had repercussions at home but served as a model for many emerging nations.

What was striking about Haughey's law reform was its humanity. This is a trait that strikes one forcibly again and again. He was a man concerned with the human side of the law and the pain and suffering of human beings who were not just statistics to him. In this area he was largely responsible for the abolition of the death penalty. 'I am psychologically and philosophically opposed to the death penalty which I think is barbaric,' he told *Irish Times* journalist Deaglán de Breadún. 'Very shortly after becoming Minister for Justice I went up to Mountjoy to see the condemned cell and I was so revolted by the whole atmosphere that I resolved to do away with the death penalty.'

Some of the other major pieces of legislation Haughey brought in while Minister for Justice were the Succession Act, the Civil Liability Act, the Criminal Justice Legal Aid Act and many others. He introduced more positive legal legislation in the short time he was Minister for Justice than had been introduced in the previous ten years.

In 1964 he was appointed Minister for Agriculture and here again he had a distinguished innings. Once more his deep feeling for and understanding of the people came to the surface. He undertook a tour of the farms of the west of Ireland, then a most poverty-stricken area. He told Deaglán de Breadún in an *Irish Times* interview:

> Up to that I had more of a tourist knowledge of the west than anything else. Then I saw the uncertainties of the situation and the conditions under which families were trying to live on small farms. That has influenced my thinking ever since. I deplore, for instance, this business of depriving small farmers of the income supplement sometimes called 'farmers' dole' which I brought about.

Here is an expression of understanding of the people far removed from the superficiality of Dublin 4, and it is worth recording that in this matter he had the full support of the Minister for Social Welfare, Kevin Boland.

When Lemass resigned Jack Lynch was elected Taoiseach and he immediately appointed Haughey Minister for Finance, the most important and prestigeous position in the cabinet. This little matter should not be overlooked. It was not Lemass but Lynch who gave him this job. There is not a shred of evidence to show that Lemass ever favoured Haughey because he was his son-in-law. If fact, there is evidence to the contrary.

Here again he distinguished himself by his deep understanding of the ordinary people, particularly the elderly for whom he provided free travel, free electricity, free television and radio licences. Perhaps his most imaginative piece of legislation at that time was income tax concessions for writers and artists. This was a great piece of legislation which is now being frustrated at every turn. I know of cases where the creative and cultural value of works have been beyond question and authenticated by the highest authorities, yet the concessions have been refused. On the other hand, concessions have been extended to works which by no stretch of imagination could be called cultural. Is it a co-incidence that many of these are British? When Haughey was introducing this legislation he said in the Dáil that when there was any doubt as to the merit of a work the artist or writer should be given the benefit. This has now seemingly been over-ruled.

In every ministry Haughey held he distinguished himself beyond question and hundreds of thousands of people today are benefiting from his legislation. Yet when the vilification started all these great achievements were overlooked.

He remained Minister for Finance until he was dismissed by Lynch in 1970 in the context of the shameful Arms Trial.

There were ten long years in the political wilderness when he had to sit on the sideline and watch the Fianna Fáil of De Valera of 1932 slowly disintegrate. But he made good use of those years as secretary of the party and travelled extensively visiting cumainn throughout the country. The high opinion of the rank and file was now such that he could no longer be ignored and after the 1977 election Lynch took him back into the cabinet as Minister for Health and Social Welfare.

Haughey was now in a safe post where he could no longer do much political harm, so there was no vilification. But this was not to last for long. Disillusionment with Lynch's leadership, electoral reverses and his seeming abandonment of Fianna Fáil's national policy caused a number of deputies to encourage him to resign well before he had intended to. The party leadership and leadership of the government was now in the ring. The two contenders were George Colley and Charles Haughey. When the day of reckoning came Haughey won forty-four votes to thirty-eight. The wheel had come a full circle. The events surrounding this election have been thrashed out over and over again but there are three elements which for some unknown reason the media largely passed over.

The first of these is that one of the principal people involved in promoting the election of Haughey was Seán Doherty. That would never be forgiven, neither by the British nor by Fine Gael, nor indeed by elements within Fianna Fáil. Doherty was destined to pay a bitter price in the years ahead.

The second element was that practically all the cabinet were against Haughey and some individual cabinet members acted in a most scandalous fashion by threatening to cut off help or support from constituencies if the TDs concerned voted for Haughey. This campaign was conducted night and day by telephone, intermediary, interview or any means deemed to be effective. Why the media overlooked that highly newsworthy item is anyone's guess. Strangely they did not later overlook similar allegations when Haughey's supporters were the alleged guilty ones.

The third element was the absolute near-panic in British ruling circles at Haughey's election. They would have been quite happy with Colley or indeed some of the other aspirants, but not Haughey. He was a Republican. He did not follow the British line on the North. Such men are dangerous. Was it at this point that OPERATION BROGUE started in real earnest?

When Haughey was elected Taoiseach he was urged by advisers to give priority to healing divisions within the party. 'Heal, Charlie, heal' was what one is supposed to have said. He accepted their advice and set about trying to forget the past in an attitude of conciliation. *This was a fatal mistake.* A surgeon does not cure gangrene by covering it with sticking plaster. Haughey should have ruthlessly amputated by simply pitching Colley and his demands to hell and insisting that each cabinet minister pledge absolutely his loyalty to the Republican ideals of Fianna Fáil and to Haughey himself as the elected leader. That is what De Valera would have done. That is what Lemass would have done. When the chips were down there might have been a few, a very few, defections but his majority was adequate to survive that. Had he taken this line of action he would have established who was master of the party and there would never have been another challenge to his leadership. The fact that he did not do so led the media to accuse him of being weak, indecisive and unsure of himself, and encouraged rebellion amongst his enemies.

I should like to emphasise this point because it concerns a

trait for which Haughey can be faulted, namely *he is not ruthless enough*. He is indeed too tolerant, too modest and too temperate with those who would destroy him at the drop of a hat. In the running of a party like Fianna Fáil, which has within it elements more at home with Fine Gael, there is no room for kindheartedness. A political party, like an army, is held together by iron discipline. One chink in the armour and it widens and spreads and ultimately bursts asunder. There is no room for magnanimity.

I emphasise very much the extreme dangers of being too nice or too soft. Elsewhere I have criticised Haughey severely for his softness with Thatcher during the hunger-strike. Had he hit her right between the eyes by sending home the British ambassador, closing the border, ending all co-operation the chances are she would have yielded. It is the only kind of language she understands. Had he done so at the time he would have won the election with an over-all majority, the trauma of the following years would not have happened, and we would not be today in the sad position of being little more than Britain's puppet. Did Thatcher foresee all this? Did she know by her intransigence Haughey would be defeated and she could be sure of a government more pliable to her demands? Look at the end result. Who gained as a result of his lack of ruthlessness? Himself or Thatcher?

Again there was the question of the transfer of Seán Donlan from his post as ambassador to the United States. It has been widely reported that he was not transferred because of the intervention of Tipp O'Neill. If that is true then it was a grave mistake to act too softly towards O'Neill. He should have been told to mind his own business. O'Neill and his colleagues have proved themselves worthless as far as Ireland is concerned. For years Irish governments have grovelled before them and what have we got? Absolutely nothing except Reagan's re-iteration of support of British occupation of Northern Ireland. It is high time we got harder and tougher. If we want an example of how that attitude pays off handsomely all we have to do is to study Dom Mintoff in Malta. He has kicked the Americans, the British and NATO in the teeth at every opportunity and did not suffer one iota. Instead he was rewarded with many billions of pounds worth of aid and investment.

But one of Haughey's greatest attributes and indeed a great attribute in any leader is his *ability to learn from his mistakes.* Recent events seem to show clearly that he will never repeat a mistake of a softly-softly approach towards the British or the Americans or his opponents within or without the party. Stalin used to say that in going forward if you meet mush keep going. If you meet steel stop. That remark is one well worth giving thought to. As a nation we have been led for far too long by jelly-fish. It is high time we showed the steel of a sword-fish. All the indications are that Haughey is shaping in that direction. His closing remarks at the Fianna Fáil Ard Fheis 1984 are well worth noting:

> Fianna Fáil offers the people of Ireland an alternative to the present state of hopelessness. Our political forebears aroused the spirit of this nation before, to overcome greater difficulties and to lead the Irish people out of more daunting situations. We are not going to be the generation of Fianna Fáil who surrendered to the *defeatest neo-colonial mentality* (italics mine). Fianna Fáil will once again lead the Irish people out of the shadows of depression in a great national advance out into the sunlight of national pride and self-esteem, progress and achievement.

After this Ard Fheis Fianna Fáil gave a reception to diplomats and press which was attended by many ambassadors accredited to Dublin, but not the British ambassador. He was simply not invited. This surely must have hinted that the new Fianna Fáil are no longer deluded and know exactly what the score is.

If this is the new Haughey, then the people will support him. They have done so before with De Valera and they will undoubtedly do so again.

I do not intend to go into the details of Haughey's subsequent career; who was for him, who was against him, who telephoned him, who changed sides, etc. The public have heard it all *ad nauseam* and they are well and truly bored.

They are now more concerned with the future than with the past; whether we are a puppet state of Britain, or whether we are free and independent; whether our youth have to live in despair, or whether there is some hope; whether our old people have to continue living in terror while our police are away protecting British interests; whether any hard-working business man can ever hope that his business will not be taxed out of existence; whether any employee can ever hope that he will have a job tomorrow or the day after. But dominating all is the question of whether we have any leader of the calibre of De Valera or Lemass who can lead us out of the depths of despair where we are now stuck.

Is Charles Haughey such a leader? Only the future can tell, but surely he deserves a chance. In the past he has proven his ability in a ministerial capacity; he has charisma and personal magnetism; he has been attacked and vilified by the media which is a great point in his favour; he has learned from the mistakes of the past, particularly it seems from the dangerous mistake of not being sufficiently ruthless. He has won every battle and routed every enemy so far, but now he is faced by the biggest enemy of all, not in a battle but in a war – a nation in the depths of despair and dejection. It may seem impossible but as he himself once said: 'The impossible only takes a little longer.' The *Irish Press* in an editorial after the last onslaught on him said:

> If ever a man showed his character in adversity it was he. . . Whatever his critics think of him Charles Haughey has shown there isn't a fighter to equal him in Irish politics, nor anyone with the obvious capacity of taking the leadership away from him in the ranks of Fianna Fáil.

If ever fighting qualities are needed it is now. In a few years time it may be too late.

OPERATION BROGUE is only resting.

Fine Gael: British or Irish?

Kevin Boland

– Is the excessive zeal in the repression of its enemies one of the main factors inhibiting real public confidence in Fine Gael of the order required for an overall majority?

– Is the complete ruthlessness in the suppression of Republicans still a fundamental part of the party's policy?

– Is the present day party dedicated to getting the people to proclaim in their Constitution that the claim to national unity is not based on the principles of democracy and justice but is a mere aspiration rightfully subject to the armed veto of a dissident minority – even when we are told that force achieves nothing?

– Do Fine Gael consider themselves enlightened realists against thick-headed diehards, the upholders of law and order against rebels and subversives, of peace against violence?

De Valera's Darkest Hour

T. Ryle Dwyer

De Valera's Darkest Hour is the story of Eamon de Valera's struggle for national independence during the most controversial period of his career. It deals with his election as Priomh Aire of Dáil Éireann, his unauthorised assumption of the title of President, his controversial tour of the United States, his obscure part in the negotiations leading to the Anglo-Irish Treaty and his reasons for rejecting the Treaty. De Valera's misunderstood rôle in the period leading up to and during the Civil War, and finally his spectacular recovery in lifting himself from the despised depths of 1923 to become President of the Executive Council of the Irish Free State in less than nine years are covered in detail.

De Valera's Finest Hour
T. Ryle Dwyer

Throughout his long career de Valera was a controversial figure but his greatest critics give him credit for his courageous denunciation of international aggression during the 1930s and for his adroit diplomatic skill in keeping Ireland out of the Second World War in the face of Nazi provocation and intense Allied pressure. His policy was guided by one paramount consideration – his concept of the best interests of the Irish people. He pursued those interests with such determination that he became the virtual personification of Irish independence.

Dr Dwyer gives a graphic account de Valera's quest for national independence. Of particular interest are well-chosen and carefully documented extracts from contemporary letters, speeches, newspaper articles, etc., giving many new insights into the thoughts and motives of this enigmatic politician, who has left an indelible imprint on Irish history.

Northern Ireland: Who is to Blame?
Andrew Boyd

– Why did Westminster remain silent while the Unionists operated a permanent machine of dictatorship under the shadow of the British Constitution?

– Why have the Southern governments let Britain hand over the lives and liberties of the minority to the Orange Institution?

– Is the weakness of Labour in the North due to the fact that neither the NILP nor the ICTU have ever had any policies that would distinguish them from the Unionists?

– What help have Fianna Fáil, Fine Gael and the Labour Party offered to the minority north of the border?

Northern Ireland: Who is to Blame? examines the events and political attitudes and ideologies in both islands that have brought Northern Ireland to its present state of dangerous instability.

The Informers
A Chilling Account of the Supergrasses in Northern Ireland

Andrew Boyd

' . . . the latest in a long line of discredited legal strategies, which included internment and the Castlereagh interrogation centres.'
Association of Socialist Lawyers

'. . . a travesty of both legal and natural justice.'
Martin Flannery, MP

'. . . the courts themselves are on trial.'
The Times, 13 September 1983

'. . . uncorroborated evidence, unsafe evidence, and dangerous evidence was being relied upon.'
Gene Turner from the US Congress

'The practice of giving immunity to the most terrible terrorists and then using their uncorroborated evidence to put someone else in prison is bound to bring the law, those who make the law, and those who enforce the law into total disrepute.'
Councillor Sam Wilson, DUP

'Most of the checks for people to prove their innocence have been done away with. I'm very concerned with the situation.'
Noël Saint-Pierre of the Québec Jurists Association

With one hand extended in what appears to be gestures of reform and conciliation and the other encased in the mailed gauntlet of repression the British have blundered through another fifteen years of political violence. Now they have turned to the use of informers.

Have the Trade Unions Failed the North?

Andrew Boyd

– Is the fundamental and universal principle of trade unions – *an injury to one is an injury to all* – completely ignored by the unions in Ireland?

– What has been the record of the ICTU in dealing with unemployment, low wages, poverty, civil rights and, above all, the problem of sectarian discrimination in employment?

– How have the unions dealt with the social and political problems of the six counties?

– Do the trade unions resent facts about discrimination in the North being published?

– Why has the trade union movement conformed willingly to the wishes of the government?

– Do the grants that unions receive undermine the independence of the trade union movement?

– What contribution has the ICTU made towards making Northern Ireland more tolerant and non-sectarian?

Do You Want to Die for NATO?

Patrick Comerford

– What would happen if a small nuclear bomb hit Dublin?

– Will Ireland be a target and suffer severely if NATO ever carries out its plans for a limited nuclear war in Europe?

– Why is Ireland considered an ideal location for missile bases for NATO?

– Is Ireland at risk because of the NATO listening system that has been placed in the seabed along the Irish coast and the use of airspace around Ireland for NATO exercises?

– Will the Soviet Union expect NATO to take over Irish facilities with or without the consent of the Irish government?

– Is the European parliament one of the major threats to Irish neutrality?

– Do   NATO and the EEC want to use Ireland as a shield?

–Is the best defence policy for Ireland to mine its ports and airports, rendering them useless to any outside force in the event of a war being threatened, and thus avoiding the principal reason for fearing an invasion?

Bobby Sands and the Tragedy of Northern Ireland

John M. Feehan

Bobby Sands captured the imagination of the world when, despite predictions, he was elected a Member of Parliament to the British House of Commons while still on hunger-strike in the Northern Ireland concentration camp of Long Kesh.

— When he later died after sixty-six gruelling days of hunger he commanded more television, radio and newspaper coverage than papal visits or royal weddings.

— What was the secret of this young man who set himself against the might of an empire and who became a microcosm of the whole Northern question and a moral catalyst for the Southern Irish conscience?

— In calm, restrained language John M. Feehan records the life of Bobby Sands with whom he had little sympathy at the beginning — though this was to change. At the same time he gives us an illuminating and crystal-clear account of the terrifying statelet of Northern Ireland today and of the fierce guerrilla warfare that is rapidly turning Northern Ireland into Britain's Vietnam.